Springtime of the Soul

Springtime of the Soul

CAROLE HAMM

Daffodil Hill Press
Lewisburg, Pennsylvania

Published by Daffodil Hill Press

Text and illustrations copyright © 2007 by Carole Hamm

ISBN: 978-0-9788646-0-6 Hardcover
ISBN: 978-0-9788646-1-3 Paperback

Designed by Keith Erdman
Daffodill art by Jeanette Sloan Campbell
Photography by Rakerd Studios

Printed in the United States of America

First Edition: March 2007

2 4 6 8 10 9 7 5 3 1

Dedicated to
Grandma Jennie
and to those
who have followed
and will follow.

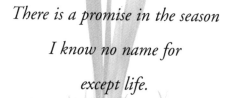

There is a promise in the season

I know no name for

except life.

—TED LODER
Guerrillas of Grace: Prayers for the Battle

Contents

Foreword

When Carole first handed me *Springtime of the Soul*, I eagerly began reading. It has been a joy for me to be a part of Carole's spiritual journey, so I was excited to see how the book would detail her story. Her unique writing style combines thoughts from the classics, the scriptures, nature, and her own personal growth.

As you will quickly come to see, Carole's favorite flower is the daffodil. Throughout the book she parallels the developmental cycle of the daffodil to the process of her own spiritual growth. Most intriguing about the book are these details surrounding her own personal growth. Her candid, transparent, personal revelations quickly point to a depth in her personal journey that will draw you into her story. Carole's personal relationship with Christ, nurtured through daily devotional times, are so captivating, you will find yourself longing for that same experience of intimacy with God. Her grasp of the deeper walk with God will cause a hunger and thirst to develop in your own heart.

After reading *Springtime of the Soul*, I realized that Carole is a teacher! It is often said that a teacher has the ability to make complex things seem simple. This is certainly true for the concepts she discusses in this book. I also discovered that Carole is a mentor! Her truths and disciplined time alone with God will function as a model for others and will speak directly to your heart.

It is my hope that as you read this book, you will either discover or renew an understanding of the awesome work of God in your life. Whether you are new on this quest for God, have been on the journey for a long time, or are still searching, your heart will be drawn to these personal accounts of God's work. I trust that, through this discovery or renewal in your own life, God will work so that you may experience a "springtime" in your soul, too.

Arlie E. Davis
Senior Pastor of Christ Wesleyan Church
Milton, Pennsylvania

Preface

In many ways, this book has been a lifetime in the making. Looking back, what I thought were ordinary events in my childhood were actually small hints of what was to come. I have a mental image of lining my cousins up on the steps behind my grandmother's house and telling them stories. I don't have any recollection of what the stories were about, but I loved telling them and adored having my cousins as a captive audience. I also remember the joy I felt when my grandmother gave me my first *Webster's* dictionary. I loved the feel of it in my hands and the scent of the pages, and the desk I received from my parents one Christmas was the best gift ever. I could sit for hours at my desk, writing and reading. I'd become so lost in the words that my parents had to call me for meals. In 1967, I spoke at my high school graduation. I was not chosen to speak because I was the smartest or the best student; in fact, I often say that I was there by default. It just so happened that the valedictorian was being disciplined for a prank he had pulled during the last week of school and a substitute was needed. In part, these were my words: "We each have a purpose in life and our [quest] is to find out what it is." Surely, out of the mouths of babes those words were spoken.

I did not realize the magnitude of those words, nor did I recall my commencement, until recently when I was invited to be the guest speaker at the graduation at our local Christian high school. As I was preparing my speech, my mother showed up at my door holding a tattered and yellowed newspaper clipping: it was an article containing my complete commencement speech as well as a photo of me. What a priceless gift she had preserved. As I reflect upon my own graduation, I believe God was already at work in my life and was perhaps prophesying what would lie ahead, but he waited patiently for me to understand his calling.

For most of my adult life, I have envisioned writing a book. Because I spent forty years owning and operating a family business, I thought it would be a book detailing my professional experiences or exploring leadership issues; I never dreamed I would write a book about my spiritual growth and the process along which God brought me—a process I feel more clarity about today, as I reflect on the past years, than I ever felt at the time I was going through it.

Over the years, my morning routine changed. Rather than unlocking the doors and getting the business up and running, I began to use the early-morning hours as a time of prayer and meditation. I not only wrote during that time, but I listened carefully to God's messages to me and began to live my life out of the direction he provided each morning. It was sheer joy to be able to rest in the presence of our Creator and write of our ongoing conversations. With my daily writings, I filled many small black notebooks. And then, while my husband, Bob, and I were on a mission trip to Guatemala with our church, I had the misfortune (or blessing) of having my bag stolen. We spent our day canceling our credit cards, reporting the incident to the local police, and making arrangements for the replacement of my passport. I was too busy throughout the day to give much thought to what else I may have packed in the bag, but that night, as I lay my head on my pillow, it occurred to me that the thieves could steal my money, my passport, and my belongings, but they could never take from me what the Lord had done within me. I immediately panicked at the thought that one of my journals had been in my bag. A sense of loss washed over me—an entire year of writing gone, an entire year of thoughts God had shared with me in our early-morning time together.

I realized there was nothing I could do about the loss of the journal, except pray that perhaps it had fallen into the hands of someone who might read it and gain something from it. Just before falling asleep, I heard a still, small voice within me whisper, "Carole, your journals will all be lost if you don't do something with them."

The next day we went to the U.S. embassy and filled out the necessary forms to reissue my passport, and then we began the three-hour drive up the mountainside to the village where we would reconnect with our group. During the trip, our host began to share with us many stories of his father's faith. How I loved hearing them! He explained that his father had written a book as a way of preserving his stories for future generations. I told him that I was very guarded in sharing my stories because I did not know how people would react to them, for they entailed events that could take place only in a spiritual world. How would people view me? Our host was quick to remind me that we must tell of the God we know, for how else will others come to know and believe in the God we love so dearly. His words struck my heart: "We must speak of the God we know."

Fortunately, when I returned home, I discovered that I had not packed my journal after all. I must have laid it out thinking I would pack it later, but then never put it into my bag. After further reflecting on my conversation with our host in Guatemala, I was convinced that I had to do something with my own journals. Thus, this book came to be. I believe this book was "birthed" within me, and so, for whatever purpose, I had to write it. I realized it was not enough simply to lock God's love within my journals and my heart; I had to share the knowledge of God's process in my life in hope that it would help others in their own growth.

If I have but one book in me to write, it would have to be a book inspired of God, by God, and for God; a book that would inspire others to seek him and know him as I have learned to know him; a book that would provide the opportunity for me to share my praises of the God I know:

*The God who loved me and performed
the miracle of life within me;*

*The God who created me and planted me
just where I belonged;*

*The God who waited patiently for just
the right time to awaken me;*

*The God who knew just what I needed
and nourished my growth;*

*The God who deepened my faith and
brought it to full beauty;*

And the God who helped me multiply his love.

My Utmost Love and Appreciation

Throughout my lifetime, God has surrounded me with the dearest and most precious gift of all, people who have loved me and been part of my journey. They have been there through various stages of my growth and provided just what was needed at the time. God does plant us right where we need to be and promises to complete the work he started in us. I declare my utmost love and appreciation to:

My parents, for giving me life and for providing me with the roots, foundation, and love that have accompanied me throughout life.

My husband, for his love and support and for his unique part in our journey.

My siblings and extended family, for accepting me for who I am and loving me anyway.

My children, who have been God's gift to me and who have taught me much about love and life.

My pastors, both on a local and district level, who helped me grow in my faith, teaching me about God's love.

My heart friends, who dearly love the Lord and who have become support for one another through love and prayer.

My grandchildren, who love their Mimi and who continue to give me hope for the future.

My many teachers, each of whom was sent my way to guide me along the path of readiness for God's glory.

Springtime of the Soul

Introduction

My beloved spoke, and said to me:
"Rise up, my love, my fair one,
And come away.
For lo, the winter is past,
The rains are over and gone.
The flowers appear on the earth;
The time of singing has come,
And the voice of the turtledove
Is heard in our land."

• SONG OF SONGS 2:10–12 •

1

I grew up in a loving and caring home. When I was a child, my parents took me to church and Sunday school and made sure that I heard the Bible stories about Jesus. I remember we said prayers at our dinner table every evening and next to our beds each night. The lessons I learned were valuable ones, and they helped me to become a person of character who has gone on to live a life filled with strong values. I knew *about* God, but I had never felt a personal relationship *with* God. Somewhere between childhood and adulthood, the world consumed me.

I married my high school sweetheart, Bob, at the age of twenty; by twenty-one, I was a mother, and my husband had signed up for a stint in the Marine Corps. Once he was discharged, we joined my father in his entrepreneurial enterprise—a restaurant and gift shop in central Pennsylvania. We worked very long hours during the early years of its development, and we loved what we were doing as well as the people with whom we worked. I never felt that we were driven by profit; we were always more committed to delivering a quality product in a clean and healthy environment. We learned a great deal during those years, and life was good to us, perhaps so good that we did not feel the need to look beyond our earthly efforts. Although from all outward appearances everything was good, it nagged at me that something was missing. In many ways, I felt I had gained the world but lost my soul. I once spoke at a local university and felt a wonderful sense of pride as I was introduced as a self-made businesswoman. But today, I cringe to remember my prideful nature, and I now know that God had his hand in our success.

Had we become lost to the "busyness" and complexities of life?

As a young couple, Bob and I were busy meeting the demands of parenthood and starting a household. We were consumed by the everyday duties of life both at home and at work. We were doing what needed to be done: changing diapers, paying the bills, coordinating our schedules, making sure the babysitter would be on time. When we were fortunate enough to have a day off, we spent it running the errands that had accumulated throughout the week. We were frenzied rushing from one event to another. By the end of the day, we were exhausted and had little energy for each other, let alone for the family members and friends we loved. We had become so caught up in day-to-day life that, like much of society, we lost sight of what was truly important.

Had we become too comfortable in our lifestyle?

We were married while my husband was still in the service, and, when he was discharged, we returned home with
twenty-seven dollars in our pockets. Fortunately, we had
jobs to return to, and we jumped right in. The very long
hours we worked enabled us to provide housing, put food on
the table, and replace our clunky old car. We were driven to
get our lives together and prove that we could "make it."
Having not been reared in privileged households, we were
enticed by the comforts we were able to afford at that point.
For once in our lives we no longer had to stack the bills up
by due date and hope that there would be money in the bank
by then to cover them. I no longer had to wait for a special
occasion to buy a new dress, and travel was not a problem.
But how many luxuries does one need? We had so much, yet
in many ways we were so empty.

Had our self-worth been tied to what we had accomplished?

For years there was always another new project, another new challenge, another new endeavor. Seeing things
come together was fun and exciting. Our plan was working:
we were meeting our goals, and the business's bottom line
continued to grow. We were proud of our achievements; we
had worked hard, so why shouldn't we enjoy the fruits of
our labors. But whenever the latest challenge was accomplished, I felt a loss to my sense of "being." So much of
what we did was tied up in our work that I wondered if anything existed outside of the business.

Weary from all the demands and responsibilities, I found myself wondering, *"Is this all there is to life? What is missing? What is the purpose? Isn't there something more?"* There was a void within me that could not be quenched by success, money, hard work, or love. I longed for something that would fill this need.

I remember spending years searching, thinking that if I looked long enough or far enough, I might find what was missing. I traveled to different parts of the country and talked with successful people in our industry, wondering if there was another avenue to follow that would bring me happiness. I had been on the slopes of Aspen, the shores of Hawaii, the streets of numerous cities throughout the United States, exploring options for myself and our business. Yet nothing seemed to click for me. One day I stood alone outside the door of a Manhattan apartment, after visiting with a wealthy investor who had great resources to offer for anything we might have wanted to do, only to realize that nothing she could provide was going to fix my personal situation. Though I did not know this at the time, I was searching for a peace that was never going to be available to me through the things of this world. There was a presence within me that had nothing to do with this earthly world and everything to do with the world beyond.

I knew that I had been born of an earthly father and mother; what I hadn't given much thought to was that I had been created by a heavenly father in his image, and that within me existed a part of him that could be satisfied only by his touch. A part of me was human, but a part of me was divine. God had placed within me everything I needed to become the person he had created for his purpose. He knew me from the inside out, and he held the mystery of my life and gently protected it for me even as I rebelled against it. He knew when the timing and conditions would be just right to begin the process. God wanted nothing less than for me to grow into the fullness of the beauty he saw in me.

During those restless years, in my attempt to find contentment I quieted my emotions with some feeble attempts at gardening. At the time, I thought it might be a way of dealing with a midlife crisis, or a pastime that would bridge the gap created by my children leaving home, but, for whatever reason, I found digging in the dirt and spending time in the midst of nature gave me solace. The much-needed activity took me outside, and my efforts were of a physical nature instead of a mental one. With my newfound love of gardening, I gradually came to see myself as one of God's flowers—specifically, a daffodil—which I embraced as a symbol of my resurrection. Just as the bulb contains everything it needs for its growth, so God placed within me all that I needed to develop into the beautiful flower he saw in me. He planted me in just the right spot, and even though I lay dormant for a period of time, he knew that the right contions would draw me forth. We have our roots planted so firmly in the ground on this earth, yet our souls strive to grow closer to the source of their life.

During the early years of my faith, I seemed to rest in the confusion of "unknowing," while God's love broke through and guided me from my lethargy to fresh understanding of his presence in me. He taught me how to reach for the light and radiance of his love and his spiritual guidance. There were times I was not aware of much movement in my growth process; God seemed to move me slowly through the various stages. But upon reflection, I can see the miracle he worked in my life and all that he taught me along the way, the summation of many years of God's love, his teachings, and his faithfulness through the many springtimes of my life.

I am and will be forever thankful for his love and patience, giving me time to search, to seek, and often to be lost in the confusion of trying to figure things out. And yet, as hard as we might try, experiencing God is nothing that we can do on our own, for it is purely by his grace. God enters from beyond, opens our hearts, and makes experiencing him possible. He desires each of us to experience the springtime of the soul, and to keep that freshness of spirit always within us, anticipating the newness of each moment with him.

The Daffodil Principle

The daffodil is a symbol of rebirth, a sign of new beginnings. There is a mystery to its growth that lies beneath the surface, remaining dormant until just the right conditions are present for it to be called forth. If you were to cut through a daffodil bulb in November, before any growth occurs, you would find within it a perfectly formed embryonic flower, complete with stem, petals, and even stamens and pistil. Until the daffodil is ready to begin its journey toward the sun, that embryonic flower remains encased and protected by layers of nourishing tissue.

God has created us in his complete and perfect form, and he waits until just the right conditions are present to bring us forth into the beauty that he knows exists within us.

Awakening

*Then you shall call,
and the Lord will answer;
You shall cry, and He will say,
"Here I am."*

• ISAIAH 58:9 •

A JOURNAL EXCERPT

Dear Father,

Lover of my soul, thank you for another springtime, another opportunity to give thanks for all that you have done in my life, another season of remembrance of my own resurrection, another morning to spend with you, one more sunrise, one more day to sit with you and feel your love. One more breath taken, filling me with your spirit and bringing me new life, the essence of all that you are.

I didn't know the blessings you had waiting for me. I knew about you, but I never took the time to seek you, and I didn't know how to find you. But your faithfulness would not allow the soul that you had created to wither and die without first being given the opportunity to come back to its Creator.

Little did I know as I drove up our driveway that spring day, years ago, how you would be working in my life, how you would transform me, heal me, nourish me, teach me, and then send me out to enter the world full of you. Help me to sing praises to you throughout my day.

Another day is dawning, and as the dark sky begins to lighten, I hear the first chirpings of the birds. Funny how nature works; they, too, know the beginning of a new day.

I hear geese honking overhead, making their way north, they are a sure sign that spring is coming! The March winds have subsided, and the last dusting of snow—the onion snow, as we refer to it here in the Northeast—has melted away. I thrill at the anticipation of the upcoming season, the mystery of what lies beneath the surface waiting to spring forth. I welcome the change that every season brings, for each holds its own special beauty. If I were to pick a favorite, though, it would have to be spring. There is nothing more refreshing than the eruption of color as everything comes alive, bursting with new growth. It's as if all of creation is awakening from a winter's sleep.

I hope this will be the last snowfall, for I long to be outdoors getting ready for the grand gala of my favorite flower, the daffodil. Is it any wonder how our hill got its name? I had never wanted to live in the country; I was a "townie" and found it very convenient to live close to all our activities. I couldn't believe it when my husband came home and proudly announced that he had found a piece of property south of town and thought it would be a great spot on which we should build. That was more than thirty years ago, and I have come to love this place of beauty, this place of retreat.

To my friends, I am known as the Daffodil Lady. And much to my children's chagrin, I'm even weird enough to have a small daffodil painted on the front of my car. I wait for people to ask me about the significance of the daffodil and am all too pleased when the question arises; it gives me a perfect opportunity to begin a conversation about my faith. It is impossible for me to approach this season without recalling one particular spring of several years ago. Then, while dealing with some difficult times, my soul was awakened and I was given a fresh start, which changed my life not only here on this earth, but also for eternity.

I'm not sure what begins the stirrings within us. Perhaps it is the need for something more, a thirst that never seems to be quenched. Perhaps we each receive a wake-up call that lets us know it's time to find that "something more" in life. Perhaps it begins during a personal crisis, when we reach a point of desperation in our circumstances. But one thing is for sure, the God who created us also placed within us a part that is wholly his, and we will continue to be restless until God and that presence within us are able to seek each other out and establish the relationship they were meant to have.

My husband and I were taking our son back to school one year after his spring break. After driving Bobby back to his dorm, Bob and I had planned to stay overnight in a hotel close to the airport, where I was scheduled to board a flight to Toronto. There I was meeting up with a good friend, and together we were flying to Japan to visit my friend's sister, who was teaching English there. At the time, I thought I was taking a much-needed vacation with a friend; in hindsight, however, I think I was running from everything that was not working in my life: a marriage that was good, but lifeless; a job that had brought success, but had consumed me; responsibilities that no longer held promise, just placed more demands on my time. Life seemed barren and dry, and I felt empty, as if I had nothing else to give.

As we set off for my son's college, I thought it peculiar that my husband suggested I drive—he doesn't exactly hold my driving skills in high esteem—but I thought perhaps he was tired from a busy week and just needed some time to relax. He did mention that his back was bothering him and at one point asked if I had some aspirin. While I drove, he slept, and my son and I talked about his spring break and the upcoming semester. He, too, soon fell asleep while listening to his Walkman,® leaving me to my driving and thoughts of my upcoming adventure.

After stopping for dinner, we drove our son on to school and, having said our good-byes, headed out to find lodging for the night. I remember that it seemed to be quite a chore for my husband to carry my bags to the room, but they were packed to the max and would have been heavy for anyone to carry. We settled in, watched a movie, and soon drifted off to sleep. Sometime in the middle of the night, something woke me. I opened my eyes to see my husband sitting in the corner of our dimly lit room; he was extremely pale and soaked with sweat. I asked how he was feeling, and he said he thought perhaps we should drive home. I continued to talk with him, and I could tell that he was in far greater pain than he let on. He was having difficulty responding to me. As I stood close to him, holding his head in my hands, I knew he needed immediate attention.

Operating on autopilot, I pulled on my clothing and dialed the front desk. As I was asking for directions to the nearest hospital, thinking I would take him myself, the young desk clerk said she would dial 911, then asked if I wanted her to come and stay with me until someone responded to her call. Only minutes later there was a rap at the door. When I opened it, there stood the desk clerk as well as the medics. I don't know how they responded so quickly to her call, but I was grateful for their speed. I could smell smoke as they entered the room, and I later learned that the three young men had just finished fighting a fire when they were called to assist us.

It seemed like a dream, my standing there watching them give Bob oxygen and take his vital signs. They moved him to a stretcher and wheeled him out of the room and down the hall, headed for the ambulance. This could not be happening to us, I thought. We were too young and had so much to look forward to. As I followed the ambulance in our car, I could see the activity inside, and my thoughts were racing: *How were things going and how was he doing? How long till we reached the hospital?*

As soon as I entered the door of the emergency entrance, I was asked to report to the registrar, just around the corner, to fill out the necessary admittance forms. The nurse went through the general battery of questions, then asked me about life-support measures and whether Bob had a living will. I was struck by fear at the implication of her inquiry.

Sure, we had our legal papers in order, but spiritually we had never prepared for death. I guess we thought we would live forever. I had never thought of life as being fragile, nor realized how quickly it could change. What seemed so important yesterday had little relevance for what we were facing today. All the material things of this world were not going to help us now.

By the time I got to his bedside, he had been hooked up to IVs and all the necessary monitors. They had begun a series of tests and were attempting to make him as comfortable as possible. He was heavily sedated and unaware of his surroundings or of my presence, but I held his hand and wondered if he could at least sense that I was there. As the doctors and nurses performed their tasks around his bedside, I kept thinking that our life together could not end like this. If we managed to get through this, we would have to work at making our relationship better, whatever that would take.

The attending nurse came in and said that Bob seemed to be in less pain and suggested that I go back to the hotel to try to get some rest. I left word where I could be reached then went to call my family. By this time, they would have thought I was en route to Toronto, and my friend would be anticipating my arrival at that airport. God, however, had a different plan for Bob and me.

The next day, the doctors verified that my husband had had a heart attack and needed to be transferred to another hospital where they could perform catheterization and possible angioplasty. They transported him to the other hospital, about an hour away, and once more I followed and wondered what lay ahead for us. We reached the hospital, and they performed the necessary procedures; for a brief time we thought that all was well, that we could head home to recuperate and life would gradually return to normal, but that was not to be. Bob became weaker and his color diminished, and I knew we would be headed for more surgery. Within a few days, I learned that Bob would need open-heart surgery in order to make a full recovery.

I remember the night before this new surgery was to take place. I was alone, away from my familiar support system, my sense of security gone, and I was fearful of what the future held. What would I do if he died? What would my life be like? God's timing was perfect: he knew this was the time I would need to reach out to him. As I lay in the darkness of my hotel room, just across the street from the hospital, for the first time in my life I felt I was in a situation completely out of my control. I did not have the answers, and I could not "fix" things. The person who always seemed to have the answers, who always was capable of making things happen, was the very one in need of help. So where could I turn?

It occurred to me to pray, but prayer was not a part of my everyday life. Yet there was no place for me to run, no one to whom I could turn, and so I found myself surrendering anyway to this rather unfamiliar process. As the tears ran down my face, the words of a prayer I remembered from my childhood returned to me, and I cried out to God, "Thy will be done; thy will be done." I had no idea of the magnitude of these few words. I uttered them out of a childlike fear, with an ignorance of their true meaning and a vulnerability I had never before exposed. I wasn't plea-bargaining my case before the Lord or asking him to make everything all right; I was willing to accept whatever was to be. Instead, I was offering myself to him regardless of what the future held.

As the words came from my mouth, I felt a sense of relief. There were no loud thunder bolts or flashes of lightning, just a quiet peace that somehow afforded me some much-needed rest. The next day seemed to drag on forever as I waited for the call from the surgical team informing me that the surgery had been successful and that Bob would be back in his room shortly. When I was able to see him, I was shocked by all the life-support equipment to which he was attached. No one is prepared to see a loved one connected to all those machines, fortunately, within a few hours they began removing them, one by one. By the next day, they had him up walking around. He was a bit wobbly on his feet, but his color was much improved, and we knew that the surgery had been successful.

By the end of the week, a volunteer was wheeling him out the front doors of the hospital and we were on our way home. (Before starting the drive to return Bobby to college, I had packed enough clothing for two weeks, just the length of time I was away. Amazingly, it seemed that God had had a hand in ensuring even that need had been met.) We were relieved to be heading home to be among family and friends and to begin our healing process. Life didn't appear to be much different than before, but our brush with death had been God's wake-up call. It took that difficult time in our lives for him to get our attention and encourage us to look beyond our earthly endeavors to his greater purpose for us. I don't know what took us so long, but I have come to appreciate that God leads us there and knows when we will be ready to reach out to him.

For a time I did not realize what had occurred that night I cried out to God in my hotel room. From my perspective, my appeal originated from my pain, but for God it must have been a long-awaited source of rejoicing. For the God I had been unable to find—indeed, did not even know I had been looking for—had found me. There could be no personal preparation for this moment, for it was purely God's love and intervention in my life. The Father who had created me had waited patiently for me, never giving up. When I needed him most, he drew me closer. During my years of searching, he had never pushed or cajoled me into receiving him. He simply stayed nearby, waiting for me. He saw greater potential in me than I did, and he desired nothing less than to awaken me from my dormancy and begin my process of growth.

It wasn't until a year later, as Bob and I sat in our pastor's office, speaking to him about receiving Christ, that I realized what had actually taken place that night in the loneliness of the hotel room. I was awestruck as I listened to our pastor provide an understanding for us about what it meant to turn our lives over to God. Truly a miracle had taken place that night. I did not understand the mystery of it all, but God had given me the perfect prayer: "Thy will be done." At that very moment, I had surrendered *my* will for *his* will. Our pastor explained to us that this new life in Christ would offer a new dimension, a dimension that would hold the mystery of the supernatural. Life would no longer be restricted to what existed on this earthly level; it would now hold the possibilities of God's unlimited heavenly power. During those days following my awakening, I was to learn much I did not know:

I did not know that, from that day forth, God would support me in my growth and draw me ever closer to him. I would no longer have to struggle through life alone, for he would be guiding me on this journey from innocence to holiness.

I did not know that he would teach me how to be in a relationship with him. He would show me, too, what a relationship should look like so that eventually all my relationships could pattern themselves after the one I shared with him.

I did not know what a relationship with God would require: that the "self" which had become so all important would have to die; that my will would become fused with his sweet, adorable will; that I would come to trust him with everything.

I did not know that as his love gradually permeated my entire being, it would radiate as well to those around me, drawing them ever closer both to me and to God.

I did not know that he would forgive me of all my past mistakes and look only to the future and to what he had planned for me.

I did not know that he would fill me with his holy spirit and that I would have access to his wisdom.

I did not know that after nourishing my soul, we would be working together here on Earth.

I did not know the assurance that he was bringing me, the assurance that the God who began a good work in me would fulfill the purpose for which he had created me.

I did not know that I no longer had to fear death and that, when my work here on Earth was complete, he would take me home to come face-to-face with him, the friend I would come to know and adore.

I did not know that God wanted more than just the mere acknowledgment of his existence, that he was asking me to enter into a covenant relationship, reuniting the soul he had created with its source of life.

I did not know that my cry, in the middle of the night, was to become an irrevocable pledge, an ever-binding agreement between the two of us, that he would be my God and I would be his beloved. "And I will establish My covenant between Me and you and your descendants after you in their generations, for an everlasting covenant, to be God to you and your descendants after you" (Genesis 17:7).

I did not know the immeasurable depth of this promise: that this covenant between us would be everlasting, that all other promises he had waiting for me would be based on this one. Oh, for the blessed assurance of his covenant, the promise of his eternal love, a love that would follow me all of my days here on Earth and then into eternity. This is a covenant I would never forsake.

*B*ut *how would I move beyond what I could see and touch to accepting and believing in a world I had never experienced? How could I build a relationship or believe in a God I could not see?*

Doing so would require my having a different set of eyes, a far different vision, a new way of seeing that can be given only by God. A. W. Tozer, in his book *The Pursuit of Man*, says, "Faith is the gaze of a soul upon a saving God. Faith is a redirecting of our sight, a getting out of the focus of our vision and getting God into focus." From the moment I said yes to God, he began to create within me a new consciousness, helping me to look at all of life in a new way. He began to nourish my soul and give me an increasing capacity to see him more clearly. No part of my human nature could bring about these results; it was truly the mystery of God's grace and mercy in my life.

My husband and I certainly would not have asked for the difficult circumstances we confronted, but we will be forever grateful for them. It was for us the worst and best of times; we were forced to pause, re-examine our lives, and begin to sort out our priorities. Without the struggle, we would have missed the joy of truly coming to know our God. I consider it a privilege to have been asked to go through the struggle.

In the midst of Bob's recovery, a friend had sent us a beautiful postcard with an image of the spring runoff over Yosemite National Park. What force, what power was depicted in that picture of water gushing down the mountainside. I could almost hear the pounding of the water as it pummeled the rocks below. The sound of the waterfalls would surely herald in the season. Her note was one of encouragement and a reminder to us not to forget, in the midst of our healing, the beauty of spring. God had done the same thing. He was able to get our attention and encouraged us to get on with the rest of our lives so that we would not miss the blessings he held for us.

After all of my endless searching and restlessness, God impressed upon me that everything I needed to learn he would teach me right where he had planted me. He had already placed within me everything that was needed for my growth, and he had waited for just the right time to bring it to life. The night of surrender had relieved the pain and fear I was feeling at that time, but the true gift God had given me would continue to unfold. The God who had awakened my soul would answer all my questions and fill every desire of my heart.

It felt great to return home after being gone for weeks. Though I had packed my bags for one trip, I ended up taking another, quite different, journey. It was the beginning of our healing—not just the healing of the body post-surgery, but the healing of our souls. We had left with an emptiness and had returned full of the possibilities of a new faith. As we drove up our driveway that day in early April, it was as if we were seeing the landscape for the first time. Just a few weeks earlier, there had been a foot of snow on the ground; we returned to the coming of spring. The grass had never seemed greener, the sky never bluer. There was a small cluster of golden daffodils blooming beside our driveway. Our landscapers must have planted them when we built the house. They had probably bloomed in that spot every spring since we'd moved in, but I'd never noticed them before. The same beauty that surrounded me that day had always existed, but I'd simply never noticed it. Perhaps I had been unable to take it in because I had never fully experienced the Creator, who had put them there for my enjoyment. The sight we beheld welcomed us home, but the true beauty of this season was still to unfold.

"Surely the Lord is in this place,
and I did not know it."

· GENESIS 28:16 ·

The Daffodil Principle

All the elements needed for a daffodil to grow from bulb to spectacular flower are contained within its protected capsule. For many long months we assume, because we can see nothing happening above ground, that the bulb is lying dormant, inactive. In actuality, however, the roots develop underground all winter long, until the temperature and the moisture level in the ground signal that the time has come for new life to begin. Narcissus, another name for the daffodil, comes from the ancient Greek word *narke*, meaning "deep sleep, or numbness."

God had allowed my roots to take hold beneath the surface and was now calling me forth, out of my deep sleep, to begin a new season of life with him.

Arising

O God, You are my God;
Early will I seek You;
My soul thirsts for You;
My flesh longs for You
In a dry and thirsty land
Where there is no water.

• PSALM 63:1 •

Dear Father,

As I read this psalm this morning, I am reminded of the early stages of my growth. How needy I was. How thirsty I was. Every part of my body was weary, exhausted by attempting to live life on my own. I was those dry bones without flesh, without breath, and without spirit, spoken of in Ezekiel. But you brought me life. "I will put My Spirit in you, and you shall live, and I will place you in your own land. Then you shall know that I, the Lord, have spoken it and performed it, says the Lord" (Ezekiel 37:14). Life would not be possible without you.

How much easier that journey became when I surrendered my will for yours. It is too much for me to comprehend the unseen mystery of your love and how it has transformed me, but I am forever grateful to you for your faithfulness and your pursuit of one of your children. Before a teaching of your word, or prayer, you breathed new life into me. You showed me your love and helped me to love myself. Each day I took the smallest of steps. Even though at times I recognized little movement, my soul had experienced your loving touch and wanted more. There was no turning back, my soul wanted nothing less than to be nourished by you. Not knowing, yet drawn, I came faithfully, truly a child of innocence when it came to knowing you. May my every breath fill me with you.

Springtime has definitely arrived on Daffodil Hill. The temperatures have climbed enough to encourage me to take my early-morning coffee outdoors as I begin making the rounds of my garden. I look upward to enjoy the clear, blue sky, and the sun warms my face. The air is invigorating and brisk, and as I sip my coffee I wrap my hands around the mug a little tighter to warm them. The chirp of the tree frogs interrupt the quiet of the morning, and I see birds busily flitting everywhere, gathering provisions to build nests in preparation for laying their eggs.

As I meander along the path, enjoying the pussy willows and the budding forsythia, I reflect on the humble beginnings of my garden. My husband couldn't understand why I had wanted to tear out all the mature plantings around our house to make room for flower beds. I had no experience with gardening, so I have no idea what possessed me to think that removing our beautiful landscaping was the right way to begin. More evidence of my increasing restlessness, I suppose. But Bob didn't question my request; he merely set about calling the professionals to give us a hand in removing and transplanting our shrubs and bushes.

I had clipped a picture of a lovely wooded area filled with daffodils from a gardening mail-order catalogue. I was positive our woods could look just like that picture. With the vision in mind, I ordered what they sold as "the works." They claimed their blend and selection, composed of one hundred large bulbs, was the best variety available and would produce an exceptional show the first year in the garden.

What had I been thinking? I hadn't dug in the dirt since the days of making mud pies with my grade-school friend Chippy. With no gardening knowledge, I had little understanding of the work that lay before me.

When the UPS truck arrived at the house one morning, my enthusiasm took over as I set out to plant *all* 100 bulbs that very day. The first few dozen went fairly easily, but as I continued in my task, it became evident that I had, perhaps, overstepped my limits. About halfway through the planting, my hands hurt, my back ached, and my knees were giving out, but I held on to the vision of that beautiful woodland and with great persistence kept plunging the bulb digger into the ground and nestling each bulb into its resting place. As I gave each mound of dirt a little pat of reassurance of things to come, I marveled at the fact that each bulb, so small and seemingly insignificant in its outward appearance, was so perfectly made that everything needed for its growth had already been placed within it. To think that each of those bulbs, simply placed in the ground and given the right conditions, would produce a beautiful flower!

As I worked in my garden, God was working within me. He had heard my cry in the middle the night, rejoiced in my willingness to seek him out, and responded by showing me his love. Understanding how the Creator and Master of All would not only hear my cry but would desire to be with me was hard. The amazing thing about this God of ours is that, even in the midst of his greatness and glory, he comes to us and says, "Let me begin with you." And that is what he did.

Somewhere in the beginning of the whole process of forging a relationship with God, I found myself asking, *Who am I?* As I looked in the mirror, I wondered if I truly knew the woman whose image was reflected before me. I'm not sure how I had become so disconnected from myself, but I felt much like Rip Van Winkle, having just awakened from a deep sleep and wondering what had happened. How had I become so lost?

I got married and became a mother quite young. Had I moved into adult life without any self-exploration? As a young couple embarked on raising a family, Bob and I had needed more than one income, so I went to work to help provide for us. Later, as we began to build a business, I simply did what needed to be done. And there was very little time for anything else. Day after day, I had met the needs of our business, but my life grew increasingly imbalanced.

I had a deep desire to know the woman returning my gaze in the mirror. What lay beneath the surface of this woman before me? What made her tick? If I spent time truly examining her, would I like who I discovered? And if I truly got to know her for herself, could I love her? My questions not only revealed a lack of understanding, but also exposed issues of self-esteem.

I read an endless number of books attempting to find some answers. My bookshelves became lined with titles pertaining to adult development, the psychology of people, the ins and outs of human relations, and all manner of self-help, but my human efforts were futile. The fine authors of these books helped me understand our human condition, and what makes us function, but they could never get to the root of my problem. Along the way I even sought personal therapy; my counselor suggested that approaching life could be compared to purchasing a sweater—try one on, and if you don't like the way it fits, then try another.

Although a lot can be uncovered and resolved during therapy, it's hard work, and for me the answers still remained vague. Try as I might, I could not break through to a deeper level of understanding of what lay beneath the surface of who I was.

We can use many different addictions to mask what we do not wish to see. We can shop too much, eat too much, drink too much, or—as in my case—work too much to cover up areas of our lives that are just too difficult to face. Frequently, we are not even *aware* of the habits we engage in to disguise our pain.

For years I had defined myself by the many roles I played: wife, mother, businessperson. But those were just my areas of responsibility. God wanted to strip away the layers that masked my identity so that I could see myself as he saw me, as one of his children. Only God knew what lay beneath all those layers that had accumulated during the years between my birth and this, the time of my *re*birth. As the Master Gardener, God holds the plan for his creation and waits for the perfect moment for the mystery of our life to unfold.

Bob's recovery was going well, and I returned to work. Getting back into a normal routine felt good. We continued to talk about our priorities and the areas of our lives that needed to change, but, actually, life didn't look that much different than it had several weeks earlier. We began to look at our schedules to see how we might reduce our work week, to find more time for ourselves and our family. Slowly sensing a need to nourish our spiritual lives, we hoped to achieve a better balance between work and the rest of our lives. Wanting to find a church in which to worship regularly, we tried several, but none of them felt right. When we told a retired pastor that we were looking for a church, he told us to be sure to find a church that met the needs of our soul. I didn't know much about my soul at that point, and I had no idea how I would know when its needs were being met.

I mentioned our search to my grandmother, whom I visited frequently at the nursing home. Immediately she began to share a wonderful story about how she and Grandpa found the church in which they worshipped for years. As a young couple, they headed out several Sunday mornings to visit churches in the valley (as she referred to their home area), looking for a church that filled their needs. She said they were looking for a church where the gospel was spoken, and when they found it, they stayed. She explained that ultimately it didn't matter *where* we worshipped, as long we chose a church in which the word of God was spoken (to be perfectly honest, I had no idea what that meant).

Through some very unusual circumstances, God finally led us to the right place. We found not just a church, but community members who opened their hearts to us and supported our faith walk. We were encouraged by their kindness and felt embraced by their love. Interestingly, we knew immediately that in this church, the needs of our souls would be met. Sunday after Sunday we heard sermons that challenged and educated us.

Then very early one morning, as I lay sleeping, I heard what seemed to be a knock at our door. It was loud enough that it woke me from my sleep. I remember waking somewhat dazed, wondering who would be coming to our door in the middle of the night. I thought I must be hearing things and so rolled over to find a comfortable position to return to sleep. But again, I heard a knock, and this time I was annoyed. Why wasn't my husband answering the door? Of course, I don't know why I should have expected him to be aroused; even when our children were small he never heard their cries. So I got up out of bed to check on the disturbance.

Cautious enough not just to open the door, I went to a side window where I could see our entranceway. No one was standing there. I returned to bed and laid down, and once more I heard a knocking. This time I thought to check the other door. But again, upon my inspection, I saw no one.

Since I was already awake and didn't want to disturb my husband, I walked to another part of the house and found a place to sit and ponder what was going on. I sat for a while and enjoyed the quiet of the darkness, then soon became sleepy and returned to bed, where this time I was able to return to bed uninterrupted. But the next night the same thing occurred. And the night after that, and the night after that. Soon, without any knock at all, I was getting out of bed, leaving all comfort behind, and sitting in the dark. I did not understand what or who was prompting me to do so, but something was fueling my inner longings.

What was I doing sitting up in the middle of the night? There I was, a busy, task-driven woman, with a block of time during which I was doing absolutely nothing. This behavior seemed so far removed from my nature. Yet night after night I sat in the dark for no apparent purpose. Then one night the thought came to me, *Could this be God?* If so, then what did he want? I found it hard to believe that the God I had shunned for many years would be so willing to come sit with me. Was he asking me to do something with this time? Surely there must be *something* he wanted of me. Oh, how blind we can be to his glory. I had no idea that he just wanted *me*. That the God whom I had always pictured as being "out there somewhere," magnificent in our universe, wanted me to sit with him and get to know him. How could this be? How could he love me enough to want to begin a friendship with me? Facing my past indifference to his love and rebellion against his presence in my life was difficult for me. I felt so unworthy of his time, yet I sensed that he was drawing me to him. Regardless of my past reluctance to acknowledge his existence in my life, he still wanted *me*. He wanted me to trust him with my life. What wonder! It was more than I could grasp.

Each morning, I would get up and walk into the darkness, not knowing exactly how I should meet him, but I came to realize that if I purposely sought him out, he would be there for me. I found it hard to be in his presence without tears; the mere acknowledgment of his closeness would begin an outpouring from somewhere deep within me. (I can't remember ever being so emotional; maybe it was my German upbringing, which taught that if things were hard, you should just get up, brush yourself off, and keep moving. This mind-set does provide some benefit, for it builds a strong character that is able to persevere during the toughest of times, but it doesn't allow for the expression of personal feelings.) I seemed to shed an endless number of tears, and I wondered where they all came from. How deep was this well, and how long would this continue? Coming to grips with the overflow of emotions that had been pushed down for so long was unsettling, but God had touched my inner being and was working beneath the surface.

Some mornings, in the midst of the tears, thoughts would come to me about areas of my life that had brought me sadness or things I had done of which I wasn't proud. God was gently helping me confront all the areas of my life that needed his attention. He was clearing the way for me, getting rid of the debris from the many seasons of my life, making ready the ground so that a new me could emerge. He was removing all obstacles before me, exposing all that I was to his penetrating light. He wanted me to become completely transparent to him so that he could show me how wonderfully he had made me. *He* didn't have to discover who I was, for he already knew: he had created me. He was, however, helping *me* find out who I was. And even though he brought to light every fault and mistake in my past, he seemed be saying, "It's okay. It's okay. I love you anyway." It is a pure act of love on the part of the lover to be blind to the imperfections of the beloved.

My outpouring of tears reflected my recognition of my inadequacies and my profound gratitude for God's forgiveness. The tears were releasing the spiritual pain of my soul and awakening my longing for God. They offered the power of purification and an acceptance without judgment; they were the expression of a transforming inner process. They surely were of a divine nature—reaching into the depths, touching the very root of the problem, and covering everything in existence with God's love.

Confronting and seeing who I was was only half the work, however. Having exposed all that was within me, God then asked me to release it and give it to him. How could I possibly release all I had held on to for those many years? Was it as simple as just saying to him, "Take it, Lord; it's too heavy for me to continue to carry." In fact, it was that simple. And how freeing it was to turn all the burdens of my past over to him. But as liberating as it was, I also felt a sense of loss. It seemed as if I were saying good-bye to much of what I knew—to past behaviors and familiar thoughts. While I mourned what had been, I looked forward to what would be. Those endless tears kept draining from me, and with them drained the hurts, the regrets, and the lost expectations of a lifetime. At the time, I seemed to be in a state of confusion, for what had once seemed so clear in my life was now clouded, and that which I had no knowledge of was coming into focus. But in retrospect, I understand that God was emptying my false self-images and the preconceived scripts of my life to which I was holding so tightly. As the space was being cleared, God was claiming my inmost parts:

God claimed my mind, so that there would be a desire and willingness to learn all that he had to teach me. He was going to be the ultimate teacher, and his wisdom would have no boundaries.

God claimed my eyes so that they would no longer be blind to his presence and would see him more clearly. He wanted me to see my past, accept the present, and anticipate the future he had waiting for me.

God claimed my mouth so that a conversation that would last a lifetime could begin between us. He wanted our friendship to grow and flourish.

God claimed my ears so that they would no longer be deaf to the soft whisperings of his sweet voice. He wanted me to be able to receive his guidance.

God claimed my hands and feet so that they would be able to do his work here on Earth. He wanted me to walk alongside him holding his hand and keeping stride with him.

And most of all, God claimed my heart so that it would no longer be hardened to his love but be ablaze with the fire within. His love would be everything to me.

God came into my life and took charge of everything so that his transforming power could perform a miracle within me. He was breathing new life into me and making me whole. My soul, which was once dead to him, was being brought back to life in him.

During this time, I experienced two dreams. I did not generally remember my dreams, so for me to awake in the morning with a vague, unexplained image in my mind was a bit unsettling. In one dream, I went to the doctor and told him that I felt something wasn't right. He X-rayed my body and reported that, strangely, there was a little, dark man inside me. I thought the dream was odd, but I didn't dwell on it. Then the following night I had another dream. In this second dream, I was standing in a doorway looking outside; there I saw the little, dark man again, only this time he was on the other side of the door walking slowly away from me.

I shared my dreams with my pastor, seeking understanding, and we spoke about my continued spiritual growth, my journey, and the concept of sanctification. He talked about the need for God's grace and his power in order for sanctification to occur, and, at the end of our conversation, he suggested that I read Romans 6, 7, and 8. As I read, I was struck by the notion of being drawn by God's love and growing into the fullness of life in Christ. And when I later looked up the word *sanctify* in the dictionary, I was awestruck at the definition: "to be set apart for sacred use, to make holy, to purify." It gave me more to ponder. Could this really be true? Was that what God was doing within me?

Romans 6:6-14 seemed to speak directly to me about the subject matter of my dream: it mentioned that our old man (or our "old self") was crucified with him, that the body of sin might be gone away, and that we had been brought alive to God in Christ Jesus our Lord. The lines described a newness of spirit brought to us by God's grace. And that, therefore, we would no longer live by the flesh but would live by the spirit, and that we were adopted and were now children of God.

To think that my body would be claimed by Christ, made holy by him, and that he would dwell within me from this day forward! I was living on Earth, but I was being introduced to a new perspective on life. Emerging from a life restricted by what was here and now on Earth, bound by purely rational thinking, I was now seeing the possibility of learning to live on God's heavenly level with his supernatural influence. Our natural world is good, but his supernatural world is best; it is the difference between living life from personal motives and living life from his greater purpose.

"To be set apart for sacred use, to make holy, to purify." To me, churches were sacred places, and pastors and priests in their work were holy. The thought of God making *me* a place of worship, making *me* holy—a person ready and available for his work—that was just way too much for my rational mind to grasp. This wasn't a topic I would read about in any self-help book on business or personal development. This was solely the work of his grace.

Although I did not understand all that was happening inside me, which will always remain God's mystery, an overwhelming peace and wholeness filled me. My body was thirsting after everything he had to offer. My soul had been touched by its Creator and wanted nothing less than to be completely filled with him. "If anyone loves Me, he will keep My word; and my Father will love him, and We will come and make Our home with him" (John 14:23). God had made a covenant promise to me to come and be in me; I believe I was making a promise to be in him. I can think of no greater way to spend my days on this Earth than to be completely filled by him.

The morning his knock interrupted my sleep brought a gift of love so full of depth and wonder that I was not able to grasp the mystery that began to unfold. If I had known then what I know now, I would have run to answer the door and welcome his warm embrace. Yes, in order to begin my spiritual journey with him, I had to leave comfort behind and walk into the dark—the unknown mystery of his world—but I would risk everything to be filled with the spirit of his unfailing love. Who would not want to receive such a priceless gift?

Perhaps we are unaware that this gift is available to us, or perhaps we do not know how to receive such a magnificent gift graciously. It is possible that we do not answer the door because of our feelings of inadequacy, our knowledge of our past mistakes, or our lack of self-esteem. We might not answer because we do not hear the knock. Most times we do not answer because of fear: fear of the unknown and what it will cost us, or fear of intimacy. But God encourages us to fear not. "There is no fear in love, but perfect love casts out fear" (I John 4:18). We must trust and have confidence in God's perfect love for us.

I had no idea how this transformation of body, mind, and spirit would ultimately affect me or where this path led, for this spiritual journey would be far different than my earthly travels. In this rational world of ours, we make all our travel plans before we even leave home. But only God would know the ins and outs of this journey, and I would have to trust him to make all the arrangements.

Since the morning his knock interrupted my sleep, I have been faithful to our time together, realizing it is the most precious time of my day. God showed me the importance of reserving time for him, of clearing the beginning of my day so that he could come to teach me, to nourish that which he had brought to life and reveal all that was needed for my growth. I used to bolt out the door, ready to dig into the demands placed before me, but he showed me how to sit quietly with him and hear how he wanted to guide my day. Each step we took together helped to build our friendship and trust. I will be forever grateful for his guidance and for the dear friend and colleague he sent my way, making it possible for me to alter my workday so that this precious time was available to me. He knew what my needs were, both spiritually and personally, and he provided for both.

My search for who I was had come to an end, for God had claimed me, and I was his beloved; there was no doubt about my belonging. Yet I had much to learn about love. We are made to love and be loved, and that is possible only if we are willing to know and be known. God's desire is to love us and bring us to our full potential—not by what he does *for* us, but what he does *in* us. This transformation is the mystery of life, how his power enters and awakens our soul and begins a process of drawing us into his sphere of everlasting love. As hard as we might try, using our limited human capabilities, we cannot alter who we are other than through God's supernatural intervention.

God's true nature is *love*: he begins by showing us his unconditional love, helps us to love ourselves, and then teaches us how to share that love with others. My focus began to shift, away from *me* and in the direction of *him*. Now that God had shown me who I was, I wanted to find out more about who my lover was.

For You formed my inward parts;
You covered me in my mother's womb.
I will praise You, for I am fearfully
and wonderfully made;
Marvelous are Your works,
and that my soul knows very well.

· PSALM 139:13,14 ·

The Daffodil Principle

For daffodils to flower in the garden in the spring, the bulbs must be planted early the previous fall, before the ground freezes—but not so early that the warmth of Indian summer will coax them into growth. A true bulb is a complete miniature of a plant encased in fleshy, modified leaves called scales, which contain a reserve of food that will nourish the daffodil throughout its growth. Daffodils prefer soil that has been deeply worked and is slightly acidic. It should be nourishing (amend it if necessary) and gritty enough to be freely pervious to moisture. Don't be afraid to plant the bulbs too deeply; one common mistake is not planting them deep enough.

The spring equinox heralds the beginning of a new season. Although it seems as if the warm temperatures signal when the bulb should begin its push toward the surface, it's actually the spring rains that start the process: water triggers the chemical reaction of photosynthesis. Once the process begins, two to three weeks pass before a small sprout reveals itself at the top of the bulb. The shoot rises and pushes away the fleshy scales as it prepares to make its way to the surface.

God carefully prepares the soil in which we are planted and encourages our growth by taking us deeper in our faith, ensuring that he brings us forth at just the right time for his purpose. He begins the process of our growth by helping us to understand who we are and from where we have come; then he summons us to where we need to go. He helps us to cast off the scales that keep us contained, that pro-hibit us from our growth, and he makes ready the path before us.

Emerging

Lord, my heart is not haughty,
Nor my eyes lofty.
Neither do I concern myself with great matters,
Nor with things too profound for me.
Surely I have calmed and quieted my soul,
Like a weaned child with his mother;
Like a weaned child is my soul within me.
O Israel, hope in the Lord
From this time forth and forever.

• PSALM 131 •

Dear Father,

Even as I write your name this morning, tears come to my eyes. My soul rejoices at the mere thought of you. My spirit is renewed as we sit together in the candlelight waiting for the new day's dawning. All that I am, all that I will be, I owe to you. You and you alone brought life to the soul that existed within me. Please continue to bring forth in me all that has been planted there by you.

To be filled up with you completes me. I could live life no other way. I have no greater desire than to come and sit with you each morning. Out of our time together, you give me just what I need for my day, for whatever awaits me. I feel embraced by your love and surrounded by your grace. It is nothing less than sheer joy. Just let me breathe you in. Is this what it means to be intoxicated by you?

May I always desire to be drawn into your presence, just as you drew me to you that first night of surrender. May I always be open to the new things you bring to me. You continue to show me the wonder of your love.

As much as I love spring, there is the reality of the winter cleanup: leaves remaining from the fall must be raked; trees and shrubs must be pruned; dead growth must be trimmed away throughout the garden. The beds need to be defined by edging, and a layer of new mulch needs to be spread to brighten things up. Just thinking about it won't get it done though, so I'd better roll up my sleeves and get started.

I make my way to the potting shed, built years ago to hold all my gardening tools. It is amazing how much equipment I need to maintain what I've planted. As I reach for the doorknob, I remember the question our builder had asked during construction: "Do you want a single or double door for your shed?" It took only an instant for me to answer, because I knew if we used anything except a single door for the potting shed, it would be an open invitation for my husband to use it for *his* equipment. No, this was to be *my* shed.

Just inside the door a corner of the shed is filled with rakes and hoes and several shovels, but for this job I needed "old faithful," my oft-mended bamboo rake, which has survived many yearly cleanups. As I drew it from the pile, I wondered if it would make it through one more season. Part of the handle had broken off, and the pronged section had been secured by duct tape for years; but I knew a new rake just wouldn't feel right in my hands. I look around for my other gardening necessity: my trusty toolbox, equipped with everything that would help me to get things in shape. My husband had given me the toolbox in my early gardening days. When my dad first saw it, he said, "Someone must really love you to have given you that toolbox." I think of myself as the lawn doctor as I grab the handle of my portable chest and head down the path in anticipation of the morning of work that's before me.

As I begin to rake the winter debris, I notice the small green shoots that have poked their heads ever so slightly above the ground: these are the first showings of my daffodils, the earliest flowers of the season. How this new growth begins, how the bulb lies dormant beneath the surface throughout the winter and waits for just the right conditions before emerging, is a marvel to me. In anticipation of things to come, I always get excited at my first glimpse of their tender shoots.

I wonder if God feels the same excitement when he sees us beginning to break through the surface of a new spiritual life. He must take great pleasure in observing our gradual and growing awareness; no doubt he looks forward to teaching us all that he has in store. Knowing what lies ahead, I'm sure he desires to provide us with everything we need in order to fulfill our potential.

Having been claimed by God and brought to new life, I thirsted for more. I wanted to know this God who had waited so patiently for me to accept his invitation to life, then had breathed new life into me. Who was this God who loved me so unconditionally? How could I find out more about him? It's as if something wanted to be birthed in me, yet I didn't know how to bring it forth. I had begun a new journey, but I didn't know the way to travel. Remarkably, all I had to do was ask the question. Once he heard my request, God began to provide the answers.

Bob and I were attending church every week, and we tried to get to the Wednesday evening Bible study as well, but clearing time in the middle of our week was still difficult. Fortunately, the pastor of the church we had begun attending made time in his very busy schedule to meet with us when we were available. The three of us would often meet for lunch. Having someone who could answer our questions as our faith slowly emerged was enormously helpful. He did not seem to mind our endless questions as we searched for understanding of things beyond our explanation, and we welcomed his time and his patience.

On one of my visits to my grandmother, I mentioned that we had found a church. Her understanding of life always amazed me; so much wisdom exuded from her frail body. She wanted to know right away if our minister preached from the scriptures. She let me know that too many ministers watered down the scriptures and that much was lost in the translation. This was coming from a woman who never missed a televised Billy Graham Crusade and who read her Bible faithfully, so I listened.

Later I remembered another dream (God seemed to be speaking to me a lot during my sleep and in the middle of the night). In this one, I was sitting across from my pastor at lunch, talking, when he looked at me rather strangely and said, "Carole, there is a name on your forehead; it is that of John." I was bewildered when I woke up that morning. Dreams can seem so real, and yet you know they're not as you lie in bed puzzled by their meaning trying to piece them together. As I got ready for work, I thought I had put the dream to rest, but such was not the case. Throughout the day my mind returned over and over to that conversation with my pastor. John, John, John: I could not get him out of my mind. What was the significance of this? Why would the name John be written on my forehead? But I was seeking a rational explanation to something that rested outside of this realm.

On my drive home from work that evening, thoughts of John were still very much on my mind, and this preoccupation was enough to prompt me to make a detour. I drove several blocks out of my way to stop at the local Christian bookstore. I was an avid reader so I had made lots of visits to other bookstores, but I had never before stopped at a Christian bookstore. Even as I parked the car in front of the store, I questioned what I was doing. I wanted to restart the

engine and simply drive away, but something beyond me
had placed me here. Hesitantly, I walked to the door and
stepped inside. The store was long and narrow, with the cash
register located right by the door. There was no way I could
get inside without having to walk right past the young sales-
woman standing at the counter.

Being much more attentive than I had hoped, she immediately asked if she could help me with something. I didn't
even know what question to ask, I was so far out of my comfort zone. Timidly, I asked if she had a book on John. I felt
so foolish standing there, in a store I had never before
entered, asking for a book on a person about whom I knew
nothing. I nearly died when she asked if I was interested in
John the Baptist or John the Disciple. Oh my, now I had two
to choose from! In that split second, all I could remember
from the stories of Sunday school was that John the Baptist
had been beheaded. I knew I wanted no part of that! So even
as my brain was thinking one thing, out of my mouth came
"John the Disciple."

She kindly led me to the shelf where there were several
books from which to choose. I don't even remember why I
chose the one I did—*The Apostles of Jesus* by J. D. Jones—
other than that it was rather short and looked as if it might
be an easy read. I wasn't familiar with the author, and I had
no idea what lay between the covers of this slim volume, but
I made the purchase anyway and exited the store as quickly
as I could. I felt I had accomplished my mission; I had
addressed the thought that had been nagging at me all day,

and now I could get on with the rest of my evening. (Boy, old habits die hard!) Later that night, though, I felt prompted to pick up my purchase and begin to read. It did not take me long to discover that the book was much more than a "quick fix" for a thought that would not go away. What I was reading had little to do with the thoughts of the mind and everything to do with feelings of the heart.

I didn't know that learning about John was going to lead me to learning about his friend Jesus, and that knowing Jesus was going to my first glimpse of God's true nature. As I read about their friendship, a fire was fueled within me. What love and affection existed between these two men; truly, they were devoted to each other. Reading about their relationship, I knew I wanted to be held in the same esteem as John; I wanted nothing less than to be loved by Jesus and known as his beloved. *What would it be like to sit next to Jesus, to be his closest friend, to lay my head upon his chest, to rest in the comfort of his arms, to live in such sweet repose? Was it possible to fall in love with Jesus just as John had more than two thousand years ago? How could I begin to build such a relationship?*

Recently, I went in search of J. D. Jones's book, which had been such an important part of my early journey. I knew it still had to be in my library, for what I had read in it years ago had made me thirsty to know more about John and his love for Jesus. As I located it and pulled the book from the shelf, I was surprised to see a Post-it note stuck on the cover; I must have had some particular purpose for placing it there during my earlier reading. The note referenced John 14. Curious about what I had read that prompted me to write the note, I took out my Bible and looked up the passage. The scripture before me reminded me of my "lost-ness" in the beginning of my journey: "…'Lord, we do not know where You are going, and how can we know the way?' Jesus said to him, 'I am the way, the truth, and the life. No one comes to the Father except through Me. If you had known Me, you would have known My Father also; and from now on you know Him and have seen Him'" (John 14:5–7).

Years ago, when I first read those words—"I am the way, the truth, and the life"—I wondered what they meant. My knowledge of Jesus was limited to what I had learned in Sunday school as a child. To me, he was a biblical figure who had shown up one Christmas night in a manger, surrounded by the angels and the wise men. He was born into the ordinariness of life, grew up the son of a carpenter, learned how to live among us, and became an extraordinary teacher to all. I wondered whether the meaning would become clearer to me as I learned more about John, his relationship with Jesus, and how he became known as the beloved disciple.

How did their relationship begin? Would it have started out like any other new relationship? A simple introduction, a shaking of hands, polite conversation; neither person knowing the other, and yet, words are exchanged between them that spark an interest, and each wants to get to know the other a little better. For these two men, it must have been a conversation about God that brought them together. Jesus, like any one of us, was looking for a loving and trusting friend, someone who wanted to spend time with him, someone with whom he could share his most intimate thoughts.

Why did he choose John? In spite of who John was at their first meeting, he came to have a pure and Christ-like soul. Jesus did not judge John; he saw him not as he was but as who he could be. Individuals who share *true* friendship see potential in each other. John was devoted to Jesus, and in return Jesus filled John with himself. Jesus' love changed John and transformed him from a man of anger into a man willing to serve. The old John was ambitious, boastful, and self-gratifying; but the new man he became through Jesus' influence was modest, humble, and yielding to God's will. The love of Jesus had infiltrated John's heart and made him a disciple of love. *A disciple of love? Is that what God wanted of me?*

I had never thought of myself as a disciple. That kind of work was reserved for those fishermen whom Jesus had chosen. But just as Jesus had chosen John centuries ago, he comes into the ordinariness of our lives today and initiates a friendship. His desire is to show us who his Father is and to assure us that he will be there to guide us through this journey here on Earth. God knew that life would be filled with trials and tribulations, and he wanted us to have a friend to show us the way. He knew that we needed his guidance, but he also knew the benefit of a soft touch and a kind word. He wanted to unite us with ourselves and others through a demonstration of his love. If he showed us how to love, in turn, we could show that love to others. If I spent time with him, would I also learn what a relationship could look like? Would his love radiate within me?

Previously I had respected and appreciated other people, but really only those who fulfilled specific needs. Of course, God never misses an opportunity; he used my time as a care-giver to my husband to teach me. My love and care of Bob during his illness and recovery taught me that true love in action is compassion.

With a heart open to the needs of others, and the example of the relationship between John and Jesus, I began thinking more about all my relationships. How was I doing in the relationships with those who were closest to me? How was I relating to my husband and my children? How about to my parents and siblings? It was never a question of whether I loved them, but I knew I could improve upon the quality of those relationships. The true test of knowing Jesus and being in relationship with him is the condition of our love for our fellow man.

He brought to me new meaning of the concept of love. Love is not something we can easily define. It can be a fond-ness shared by people who enjoy spending time together due to similar interests or shared experiences. It can be an expression of deep affection. It can be the strong attraction fueled by chemistry, which exists between two people entwined by romance. As humans, we are limited in our understanding of love, but knowing God and feeling his unconditional love surround us is what makes our growth in him possible. He didn't seek me out for what I could do; he came to shower me with love, freely given, and asked nothing in return. God showed me that his true nature is love, and that we are made in his image. We cannot begin to fathom the breadth and depth of his great love for us. Nor can I now imagine life without him, for once my soul was reunited with its Creator, its source of life, the bond we shared could never be broken. Without this union, my soul would surely have perished and missed out on the beautiful opportunities attainable through spiritual growth.

For years, I thought my coworkers should leave their problems at home and come to work free of distractions. But I began to understand that asking them to do so was, in effect, encouraging them to bring only part of themselves to the workplace. I began to wonder what would happen if I were to take an active interest in their lives and listen carefully when they spoke about what they were experiencing in their personal lives. Before this shift in my mind-set, I would have called this behavior meddling, but I now began to see it as a new way to reach out to others. I developed a genuine concern for my coworkers' well-being. Though I remembered learning about the Golden Rule, "Love one another" took on a different meaning after reading and learning about Jesus. It became a matter of loving even those with different lifestyles or beliefs and showing love to people who weren't always my favorites. It's easy to love your best friend, but it's harder to love someone who has done you an injustice. It also meant opening up to the pain and suffering of others, and being able to show my compassion to them. How different our world would look if we could simply meet people just where they are, without judging them or their circumstances, and show them our unconditional love.

I would meet and talk with a lot of people during the course of an average business day, and my conversations virtually always revolved around work. I was generally preoccupied by whatever was the task at hand, and I took little time to connect with anyone at a deeper level. But soon, I became irritated with a diet of exclusively "surface" talk. I hungered for more than what just a quick hello could offer. I was starting to realize that work relationships were every bit as important, if not *more* important, than the work itself. I also wanted to conduct my participation in daily exchanges in a kinder and gentler manner so that I would become more approachable to others. All my communications began to take on a greater sense of richness when during each exchange I started to ask myself, *"What would this conversation be like if I were talking with Jesus?"* When the soul is the director of our words, then what comes out of our mouths is truly what rests in our hearts; all communication then becomes an act of love. A very wise friend and counselor once advised me to schedule only 50 percent of my time, realizing that the other 50 percent would become the true work of my life, the work God placed before me, the work involving the people around me.

What else was Jesus teaching John? Jesus was teaching John the principles by which we should live. Jesus knew that life consists of the outward actions of our inner thoughts. Our lives progress as a result of our thoughts, and those thoughts are best influenced by remaining in God's presence. Jesus took everything before the Lord and asked for his guidance. He sought his counsel not so much from man, but from his Creator, who knew him best and knew the path he should follow. Prayer preceded all of Jesus' activities. He rose early every morning for prayer and went off every evening after dark to pray in private. No wonder Jesus could perform all those miracles; all of his thoughts were touched by the magnificent wisdom of his heavenly Father! What if all matters of our everyday lives were taken before God? Imagine how he could influence our personal struggles, family conflicts, and our work considerations.

God had commissioned Jesus to find others who shared the same love for him and who would be willing to spend their lives sharing their faith with others who did not yet know him. He knew that Jesus would need people who were faithful to the task that would be forever before them. There was work that needed to be done here on Earth, and Jesus could not do it alone. The work would need to be sustained when Jesus was no longer here in person. Could continuing the work Jesus began be the greater purpose for our lives? If so, what was the reason for God's continued grace working within me? Was his continued purification bringing me into his holiness?

John showed himself to be faithful; he left the life to which he was accustomed to enter a new reality. He left the known to enter the unknown; along the way he experienced forgiveness, healing, and profound love. He had no idea where he was going, but he trusted Jesus with his life. He didn't have to go, but he yearned to be with Jesus and was drawn to him. John renounced all that he was and followed Jesus in utter love. Jesus, in return, helped John re-create his life, and that new life was rich and whole, making faith possible. Jesus helped him to see that the human condition and our daily circumstances were not burdens, rather opportunities to influence those around us. Could I do the same?

Through his many lessons, Jesus taught us about love, relationships, and the right way to act toward one another; his greatest gift of all, however, was the gift of himself. We may not remember all that he said, but we will remember who he was and what he did. He cared little about the needs of his own life and everything about the needs of others. His entire life and even his death serve as an example to us. He was brought to Earth to connect us with his Father and help lay down a foundation for the lives of all future generations. He showed us not only how to live here on Earth, but also how to prepare for our eventual death and eternal life with him. We would all live differently if we could see that our earthly life is simply preparation for the full reunion of our souls with the God who created us.

When I think back to the day that I was compelled to stop at the Christian bookstore downtown to find a book about John, I can't help but be thankful that God didn't let me restart the engine and drive away. He walked with me into the "unknown" that day, when I could have easily run from what he had called me to do. And what if the salesclerk had not been there to support my inquiring heart? I could easily have exited had she not been so attentive as soon as I entered the store. A number of circumstances could have interrupted my growth, but God made the way possible.

God comes to us and is able to make all things new. Just as he was able to make a new man out of John, he is able to re-create each of us and wants us to live a life anew with him. He also wanted John to know that he was the source of all things in his life. Jesus taught John that life begins in God and ends in God. John lived to be a very old man. There was much in his life in which he could take great pride, for he was accomplished in many areas, but the thing he was *most* proud of was his friendship with Jesus. If he had stayed behind, he would not have learned how to believe. I, too, wanted to be a believer in Jesus and follow him, to have him show me the way.

By this all will know that you are My disciples,
if you have love for one another.

· JOHN 13:35 ·

The Daffodil Principle

O ut of the capsule come the roots to drink, the leaves to feed, the stem and flower to mate. The stem probes upward, sometimes within a hairsbreadth of the soil's surface. Remarkably, it may halt its progress if it detects the danger of falling temperatures. Its growth will then resume when the conditions improve. For this reason, we don't have to fear the effects of a late frost on our bulbs. Regardless of the impending threat, the bulb has the ability to hold back and continue its growth later. As fragile as we may think the daffodil to be, it remains quite hardy-laughing at the inclement weather conditions possible throughout April.

God will protect us against the harshness of this world and continue to show us how to proceed with our growth. Even if we stop short of our breakthrough, he will see to it that we resume our development when the conditions are right.

Unfolding

So He humbled you, allowed you to hunger,
and fed you with manna which you did not know nor
did your fathers know, that He might make you know
that man shall not live by bread alone; but man lives by
every word that proceeds from the mouth of the Lord.

• DEUTERONOMY 8:3 •

A JOURNAL EXCERPT

Dear Father,

As I wipe the moisture from my eyes, I wonder what you have in store for me today. What mystery will you unfold? With your word open before me, I think this is all I would need. You strengthen and fortify me against all the trials and tribulations of this world. Before surrendering my life to you, I lived out of anxiety and worry, but now I rest in your hands knowing that what you bring to me is just what I need. The manna that you send from above is just the right portion, just right for the day. I cannot save it, so I must use it up today. So let me consume it, knowing that you will be back tomorrow, filling my every need.

Help me to be filled with your life-giving presence so that all of my actions will be guided by you. Let me delight myself with your commands for my day, knowing that whatever you ask of me will bring joy to my heart. I know that my path will be made clear and my soul strengthened for the journey.

Blessed be your Word. Let me remain in you…remain in you. Your presence is all that I need. I wait for your direction and guidance for whatever lies before me.

Now that the winter debris is cleared away, things are beginning to shape up rather nicely. What I have missed with my rake will be taken care of by Mother Nature; she is sending the spring rains to melt away the last of the existing snow and wash off all the surface dust from the landscaping and surrounding garden areas. With each passing storm, there is a noticeable difference in the shades of green around the hillside. Almost daily I can see the change that the rains and the warm sun are producing. The grass has turned from a drab brown to a forest green, and there are signs of new growth popping up everywhere.

As I make my morning rounds, I stumble over a few small branches that have been blown down by last night's storm. When I bend to pick them up, my eyes catch sight of the daffodils. It seems as though they have grown inches just since yesterday. I know that is not possible, but the warm sunny days are bringing them forth. I thrill at the thought of how this hill will soon be bathed in a sea of yellow. I pray that another snowstorm doesn't come in the midst of their growth, or that a cold morning frost doesn't ruin the prospects of the coming season unfolding before me. The tender stems need the warmth of the sun to power the process of their growth.

There are a few daffodils that I notice are just getting ready to break through the surface, I stoop over and, with my index finger, gently loosen the dirt from around their stems. It takes such little encouragement to help them finally break through the surface to find their source of light waiting for them. The rains had come, sending the right signal for their growth to begin, and the warmth of the sun had encouraged them to leave their comfortable resting place deep in the soil and to journey upward to new life above ground. I can imagine myself being that small shoot coming out of the ground and God's finger gently reaching down and clearing the dirt away, moving it slowly off to the side, allowing my growth to continue.

Week after week, we returned to the church to hear the sermons. Each sermon educated us in the ways of the Lord and how he wanted to come to work in our lives. Some made us cry, some made us laugh, and some really dirtied up our shoes, convincing us that there were areas in our lives that needed our attention. Our pastor had a gentle way of challenging us and bringing a new reality to our thinking. We were discovering that God's presence was not limited to Sundays, but needed to be carried forth into our everyday living. Grandma Jennie was pleased to hear we had found a church and were attending regularly.

As my soul was emerging, God knew exactly what I needed to be drawn into his light and was faithful in provid-

ing me with the nourishment. I stand in awe of God's transforming miracle within me. Somewhere in the vastness of
the universe, God heard my cry and met me in my hour of
need, he accepted me just as I was, forgave all of my mistakes and began demonstrating his love for me, showing me
that I was worthy of being his beloved and receiving the
many gifts he had waiting for me. He claimed me as his very
own, filled me with his spirit, and introduced me to his son.

As God was bringing forth the mystery of my life, he
continued showing me the way. I found myself faced with
more nagging questions: *What is the basis of our faith?
Where did I need to go to learn more?* I thought perhaps I
should return to the Christian bookstore, where I hoped that
he might once again direct me to answers for my searching
heart. I was gradually learning to listen to his soft voice
whispering gently in my ear. I became much more aware
each time I heard these quiet "nudgings," and slowly my
trust in his guidance grew; each time I followed his recom-
mendation, he provided me with more answers for my life.

My trip to the bookstore was a little easier this time
around; although I still felt awkward, I didn't have the same
fear. My purpose for being there was somewhat clearer, but
my knowledge of the selections available for reading was
still quite limited. As I stood before the many books lining
the shelves, my eyes caught hold of a daily journal/devo-
tional, *My Utmost for His Highest,* by Oswald Chambers. I
liked the sound of the title: *utmost, highest*—those words
certainly spoke of stature. Again, not knowing anything

about the author, but liking how the journal was arranged, with each day offering a scripture reading and a place to write, I thought this book might be just what I was looking for. The journal became my daily companion and guided my thoughts for an entire year. Each day I would read a lesson, reflect on what it was saying to me, and then write down my particular feelings about the passage. It was as if a conversation had taken place between the author and me. Though no spoken words had been exchanged, I felt as if I was engaged in a dialogue with Chambers himself. Little did I realize that his book was a Christian classic and had been a bestseller since 1935. As I worked my way through the journal, I was being introduced not only to the dynamic writings of Oswald Chambers, but also to God's many biblical truths. Like the apostle John, I felt I was learning how to live in Christ.

Before I completed all 365 lessons, I felt prompted to supplement the work I was doing with *My Utmost for His Highest* with some forays of my own into the Bible. It had been years since I had picked one up. My best recollection of the Bible was from vacation Bible school. How well I remember listening to the many stories our teacher told and working diligently on the crafts that we were then allowed to take home. I am thankful today for the faithfulness of those teachers, who came every day to a group of youngsters to share their knowledge of the gospel, and for parents who felt it was important for us to hear these stories.

As much as I had loved hearing the familiar, old stories as a youngster, as an adult I never made the Bible an important part of my life. I was an avid reader and read for pleasure as well as knowledge: the books on my shelves ranged from self-help to gardening to biographies. I knew that if I went searching, I would likely find a Bible somewhere in my collection. Sure enough, there it was, in a forgotten corner of one bookcase, beneath a few layers of dust. It hurts my heart, even as I write this, to think that the most valuable book of my life sat for years on a shelf, just waiting to be rediscovered. I carefully wiped the dust away and considered: God had begun a friendship with me and was continuing to draw me to him. *Would my exploration of the Bible be another way for him to converse with me? If I were to become a disciple of love, would the truths written in this sacred book provide me with what I needed to know? Would they help equip me for the sacred purpose he held for my life?*

I sat down and, with my traditional mind-set, opened the Bible and began to read. I don't know what I was thinking. Was I going to read it like a novel, from cover to cover? Was getting through it yet another project, just one more task I had to complete? As I scanned the pages of Genesis, the story seemed rather dry and irrelevant to my life. Perhaps the New Testament would be easier than the Old. And then I thought about Jesus' friend John; perhaps that might be a better chapter with which to start. It wasn't long before I realized there was something quite different about the Bible. It was a library all in itself. Every book I read held a special education for me about the history of an ancient people—their stories, their praises, their songs.

I found I could read it like no other. We are taught to read for information, but my experience exploring the Bible was different. My reading of it seemed to occur at a different level; I was not engaged in the rational, cognitive thinking I was used to. This was like reading, but not reading. Someone mentioned to me that exploring the Bible was like "hovering" over his word, and I found that to be a rather apt description. I learned to allow myself to linger for a while with the words that were before me, not anticipating any particular direction of thought, but giving myself permission to let the words soak into my consciousness and my heart. It wasn't long before I found myself falling in love with the book and its many authors, all of whom had taken the time to share the stories of their lives, to preserve the events of their day and their faith for all who followed. I could feel the spirit of those men and women. Their stories came alive as I read about their pain, their suffering, and their joy. I began to see them as real people, imperfect, lonely, and at times fearful.

When I took the time to sit patiently with the words before me, not rushing to reach the end of a chapter, not attempting to draw conclusions, I discovered that certain words or phrases would catch my attention and cause me to stop and ponder. There was a certain rhythm to what I was doing. I'd read, then reflect and pay attention to how the words were speaking to me, letting them draw me to them. On one level, I was simply reading someone's life story; then I wondered what I would have felt if I had been there with him or her; finally, I questioned how these words were speaking to me today, how they were relevant to my life. It is the mystery of God how the print on those thin pages, written so long ago, is able to enter our consciousness and work within us; how, once we reach a quietness of spirit, our soul will hear God's voice at an even deeper level.

As a friend and someone who wants us to know him, God yearns to speak to us. How else will our relationship with him grow? The Bible is not merely a record of historical events or a transcript of what God said so long ago; it is a living book that continues to speak to us as clearly and profoundly today as it did to those of an earlier time. He is speaking to us today, as he did yesterday and days before. God desires to speak to our hearts and minds; if we believe that he is articulate in his universe, we will understand that the truths in the Bible endure forever, are relevant forever.

Thomas Merton wrote a book titled *Opening the Bible*. Though short, it offers great insight into the Bible. Merton writes: "The basic claim made by the Bible for the word of God is not so much that it is to be blindly accepted because of God's authority, but that it is recognized by its transforming and liberating power. The 'word of God' is recognized in actual experience because it does something to anyone who really 'hears' it: it transforms his entire existence."

We may open the Bible and read over the words in front of us, but if we "hover" over them and genuinely allow them to soak into our being, the Bible will open us to further changing our hearts and our lives. The mystery of how the Bible achieves this transformation within us is not for us to know, but it occurs. Quietly, remarkably, profoundly, the Bible transforms those who read it and truly "hear it."

I do not begin to understand how words recorded thousands of years ago can speak to us today, but as I began my own reading of the Bible, each day I grew more certain they were speaking to me. If I would simply come and sit with his word, God would give me just what I needed for my day.

His word became my counselor and my teacher. If I had done or said something that needed his interpretation or clarity, he showed me. He revealed truths about me and often asked me to consider a given situation with a different mind-set, one that placed him in the center of all things. His reprimands were gentle, and I did not mind the corrections. He always showed me how to change habits that were not of his character; in this way, he was bringing me into a right relationship with him.

His word lifted my spirit and encouraged me; no matter the circumstances, he gave me much needed hope as I struggled with and through life, He became my lifeline. God entered into my life precisely where I was, even if I was caught up in the minutia of the day, he was there to oversee the smallest detail as well as the most major decisions. Nothing went unnoticed.

His word strengthened me for the work that was before me. As I read, he gave me the wisdom and courage to say the things that needed to be said, to take the actions that needed to be taken, and to see opportunities where previously I could see none. He helped me realize that our ordinary lives are sacred and that we play a vital part in the fulfillment of his promises.

His word was my first introduction to prayer. As I read and pondered Bible passages, just being present to the phrases before me led me into worship, into times of communication with God. They became opportunities to praise him and give him thanks, and sometimes simply to sit in awe of him.

His word is another way of learning about God. The Bible is God's truth; it directs us toward a greater love of him while simultaneously creating within us a deeper love for others. Oh, for the saints who have gone before us, who recorded not only the events of their day but also their love of God, creating, as they did so, the greatest book ever written, the greatest love story ever told. The Bible is truly a love letter, preserved to be read and reread throughout one's lifetime and by every succeeding generation. We were made to love and be loved, and that is possible only if we are willing to know and be known by him.

Whenever my time with him came to a close, my soul was always refreshed, full, and complete—ready for the day. The conversation that had taken place in the morning went with me throughout the day and kept me on track regardless of what the world had in store for me. His divine word would fill me and continue to transform my mind and my soul as the hours passed. As I sat with him, he gave me direction: sometimes letting me know there was someone to whom I needed to apologize, sometimes suggesting someone to whom I needed to speak or write. And my willingness to do the work he gave me invariably brought richness to my daily existence. Not wanting to miss a single command or instruction, I would sit with my "command book" and write down all that he brought to mind. He who believes is obedient; he who is obedient believes.

This is what D. L. Moody had to say about the Bible:

Take the Bible: study it; leave criticism to the theologians; feed on the Word; then go out to work. Combine the two, study and work, if you would be a full-orbed Christian. The Bible is assailed as never before. Infidels cast it over board, but it will always swim to the shore. The doctrines, the promises, the messages of love are as fresh to-day as when first spoken. Pass on the message; be obedient to commands; waste no time in discussion; let speculation and theorizing in to the hands of those who like that kind of study. Be willing to do little things for the Master (*The Life of Dwight L. Moody by His Son*).

When my day was over, I not only prayed for the goodness he had given me but for another morning just so I could be with him, so I could continue to receive his direction. He supplied the manna for my every day. His manna is to heal us, teach us, and guide us; it cannot be saved for another time, for manna perishes—he wants us to use it that day. "This day the Lord your God commands you to observe these statutes and judgments; therefore you shall be careful to observe them with all your heart and with all your soul. Today you have proclaimed the Lord to be your God, and that you will walk in His ways and keep His statutes, His commandments, and His judgments, and that you will obey His voice. Also today the Lord has proclaimed you to be His special people, just as He promised you, that *you* should keep all His commandments" (Deuteronomy 26:16–18).

There are so many riches that await us in God's sacred book. Emmet Fox, in the preface of his book *The Sermon on the Mount: The Key to Success in Life*, describes the study of the Bible as not unlike the search for diamonds in South Africa: "At first people found a few diamonds in the yellow clay, and they were delighted with their good fortune, even while they supposed that this was to be the full extent of their find. Then, upon digging deeper, they came upon the blue clay, and, to their amazement, they then found as many precious stones in a day as they had previously found in a year, and what had formerly seemed like wealth, faded into insignificance beside the new riches. He goes on to encourage us in the exploration of Bible Truth, to see that we do not rest satisfied in the yellow clay of a few spiritual discoveries, but that we should press on to the rich blue clay underneath."

The wealth that awaits us between the covers of God's sacred book goes on into infinity; we can never possibly mine them all. It didn't matter how often I returned to the same passage; each time I would read it, I would be affected in a different way because of where I was in my growth, my understanding, or my need. What we read today will not be what we read tomorrow, for as our faith grows we will understand it differently. We will change and grow, but his word will remain constant.

As we read, his divine word touches us and transforms us in a way reserved only for the divine Creator. Thus is the power that transcends the soul that is and was created by Him for the purposes of this earth. May we find new birth in the words that he has left behind for us to cherish and hold dear. We may come to fall in love with the one who loved us first and who holds the key to how we are to live our lives.

To think that God's manual for the growth of my soul had been within such easy reach and yet had remained unopened. I regret that I didn't begin to make it a priority earlier in my life, but I am so thankful that God didn't let me miss out on the treasures that he had waiting for me between its covers. Our spiritual growth requires God's word for his spirit-given wisdom. His word sustains us in this world. Let us be rooted in his truth and love; and let us trust him with our life, with our entire body, mind, and soul. May our one desire be for him to know us and may we entrust ourselves to his way. If I were to follow him, and have him be the Lord of my life, I would have no other way of knowing him than through his word and his commands.

Since locating the first Bible on my bookshelf, I have purchased and read from several Bibles, and I have claimed each one of them as my own. As I have spent time in his word, I have underlined, highlighted, and written in the margins. When I went back and thumbed through the pages, the thought came to me that, as I was reading about God's history, the stories of Jesus and the miracles he performed, God was writing *my* history. It was the story of my life and the miracle he had performed in me, the recorded events of my life lived out of our covenant relationship, his work in me and my response to Him. He spoke to me through His word and I remained obedient. He guided and directed my life through our continual conversations over the years. Our mornings together had become the spiritual journey of my soul as it had traveled since being brought to life. It was a journey of my becoming all that he saw in me.

My journey continued, and so did my tears. No longer gushing, they were more sporadic, and they came when I least expected them. I didn't know if I was more concerned that they would never stop or dismayed at the idea that they might stop. I asked my pastor about my reaction to the tears, and he replied, "Carole, don't worry. Your tears will only take your faith deeper."

"For the word of God
is living and active,
sharper than any two-edged sword,
piercing to the division
of soul and spirit,
of joints and marrow,
and discerning the thoughts
and intentions of the heart."

· HEBREWS 4:12 ·

The Daffodil Principle

The stem, leaves, and flower all make their way to the surface simultaneously. As the tender shoots begin to appear through the soil, sunlight strikes the leaves and powers their growth through the process of photosynthesis, which literally means "put together with light." The leaves act as a miniature factory, taking carbon dioxide from the air and combining it with water and sunshine to manufacture useful starches and sugar needed for growth. The elements necessary for the daffodil's growth include light, temperature, water, humidity, and nutrition. The environment directly affects how well the plant grows; anything less than ideal restricts its ability to flourish.

We are drawn to our source of life, and God nourishes us by the light of his word. Staying close to his word brings light to our path and builds a firm foundation for our faith. We must abide in his word in order to grow.

Unfurling

Call to me and I will answer you,
and show you great and mighty things,
which you do not know.

· JEREMIAH 33:3 ·

Dear Father,

As I light the candles in preparation for my time with you, I think of how the flame has been a symbol of your light in my life. You bring light to the darkness. The warm soft glow is a reminder of your presence and your love. You have guided me and shown me how to live out of your light. It is sheer joy to sit with you.

I remember the night as I cried out to you, "I don't know how to pray," and you sent the words, "Thy will be done, thy will be done." How often I have thought of those words and how perfect they were. Those words return to me frequently and are a reminder of our initial encounter. To come closer to you is to go deeper in prayer. It is often in the silence that I find you. Help me to sit and wait for you.

You gave me the example of your son, who prayed in times of joy and in times of pain. His life was prayer. He came to you in all things. Help me to bathe all that I do in prayer.

Over the years I came to learn many things about the endearing daffodil bulbs. When I first began planting daffodils on our mountainside, I was afraid that the animals of the forest would find them and dig them up. I was pleased to learn that the daffodil is one bulb with which they do not care to bother. The squirrels would dig up other bulbs and carry them away, but never that of the daffodil. I'm not sure why wild animals do not consider them a favorite, but it was reassuring to know that once I spent the time and effort to place them in the ground, they would be safe from becoming someone's food for the winter.

These beauties required much less attention than my annuals and perennials, for they were programmed to return year after year and during their growing season they required no hoeing, no weeding, no spraying, and no pruning. They were also very forgiving of the planter. It didn't seem to matter if the quality of the soil differed from location to location on the mountainside. As long as the soil wasn't too wet, the bulbs flourished. Even when I neglected to place additional fertilizer around their base, the bulbs were able to get the nourishment they needed. But there was something even *more* amazing that I was to learn about these bulbs: if they are not planted deep enough, their roots will pull them deeper. So it was with my faith.

Bob and I continued to meet with our pastor over lunch about once a week, and we began participating in a few of the activities at the church. Bob was assisting with some building designs and plans for a new sanctuary, and I made myself available in an ad hoc capacity. In other words, I wasn't able to spend much time on any specific committee, but I was willing to be used as a resource for any of their needs.

I continued going to the nursing home to visit my grandma, and one evening as I was preparing to leave her room, she caught me by surprise when she commented that she didn't know why she was still alive at 92. I was at a loss of words, and I wasn't sure how to console her. I stooped over to give her a hug and kiss her good-bye, hoping that this wasn't a sign of her final adieu. It wasn't till I was halfway down the hall that I realized that her single greatest purpose for being there may have been to continue to share her faith with me. She did not understand, nor did I at the time, how crucial she was in supporting me during my spiritual growth. Regrettably, I did not share this insight with her; if I had, I like to think the notion would have given this time of her life greater purpose.

God, too, was doing his utmost to sustain me and bring me into his fullness. From the moment my soul was reunited with its Creator, the process of growth began. His unconditional love had drawn me closer to him, and our friendship had deepened through our mutual trust. Because God is not of this world, he has to find other ways for us to communicate with him. First, he introduced me to his son, who taught me about becoming a disciple of love. Then, he taught me to come sit with him and spend time in his word, allowing it to speak to my heart. And next, he was going to teach me what prayer was about. Just as I had lacked knowledge of both Jesus and of his word, I also knew little about prayer.

In our household, my siblings and I said grace before family mealtimes and before going to bed at night. We always uttered from memory the same childhood prayers at these times. I also recall attending church and saying the Lord's Prayer in unison with the rest of the congregation. Sadly, all these prayers became routine for me; I said them without much thought to the meaning the words held. For some reason, I grew up thinking prayer was something one said out loud and from memory. I never understood how personal and intimate prayer could be.

As Bob and I attended more functions at the church, I heard people pray publicly with great strength and eloquence. I wondered what it took to be able to pray in that manner. I would sometimes be invited to pray with others in small groups, and at these times I felt inadequate, needing to search hard to find appropriate words when it was my turn to share. Was it that I was not yet a *mature* Christian? Or did I not yet have a depth of faith that would allow me to share at a deeper level? Perhaps I just needed to learn a certain technique; prayers often seemed to follow a simple three-step formula: "Knock and it shall be open to you, seek and you shall find, ask and it shall be given unto you." But I did not know what to ask for. Should I simply ask God to show me how to pray? Should I ask that he take me deeper in my faith? As our relationship grew, there was an insatiable desire within me to come into closer union with him. Never once, if I asked in his name, did he not respond. And God chose to teach me about prayer in a very personal way.

One summer evening, as I pulled into our driveway after a busy day at work, I was struck by the beauty of a colorful sunset casting its brilliance through the trees behind our home. I parked the car, got out, and began to gather my belongings from the backseat. It had been a long day. I was tired and wanted to go inside, change clothes, and relax for a while. But as I started to get my things together, my eyes once again caught the beauty that was before me, and something in me was being drawn in the direction of the sun's rays.

Reluctantly, I walked from my car and up one of the paths into the woods. Soon I was standing at the edge of the tree row, gazing out over the valley, watching the sun as it dipped ever so slowly behind the mountain ridge and left its trail of faded colors behind. I felt honored, as if the beauty of this entire panorama had been created for the enjoyment of my eyes only. There was no one else around to witness this grand show of nature. I don't know how long I stood there, but the longer I stayed, the less I wanted to leave. I found a nearby stump and sat for a while.

My mind began to clear of the thoughts and responsibilities of the day, and I entered a world all of my own. The only reminders of the outside world were the noises that drifted up from the valley. I could hear the voices of small children playing in a farmer's field and a truck shifting gears on a nearby highway. From above came the muffled sound of an airplane engine. Even these interruptions soon drifted away, and I was then engulfed by the evening activities of the woods.

A young deer, making its daily journey back up the mountain, walked toward me. If he had picked up my scent, he made no quick motion to run away. He looked in my direction, and I felt he might be acknowledging the fact that we both belonged here. Behind me came the rustling of leaves, and as I looked over my shoulder, a young squirrel leaped into the air and scampered up the bark of a tree. As the day continued to draw to a close, all activity gradually began to cease. Even the chirping of the birds subsided, and all of nature seemed to know that it was time to put this day to rest. What nourishment this silence brought to my soul! God is a bit of a trickster, for he had drawn me to this place by its physical beauty, but then he showed me the richness that comes from remaining in his silence. God seemed so present here. With no interruptions and in this setting of nature, I was able to come and feel his love and let him know that I loved him in return.

I sat until all the sounds of the day had come to rest and the light of day had disappeared. It was only when darkness came to the woods that I made my way back along the path, took my things from the backseat, and went inside.

Throughout the summer and early fall, I returned many times to this spot. It became the clearing area not only for my mind but also the clearing area for my heart. Whenever I visited the stump along the edge of the tree row, I knew that God would be present; much like the sunset that I viewed from there each evening—sometimes brilliant, sometimes shrouded by clouds—his presence was guaranteed. What a welcome joy to walk into the woods and arrive at a place where I was completely accessible to his love and open to receive all that he had to offer.

He was teaching me that the deepest of my prayers were achieved when I was willing simply to be with him, totally in his presence, without pretense. To be emptied of all thought and to have my heart be completely open to hear him. Richard Rolle, author of *The Fire of Love* (written in 1343), says that true prayer occurs "when we do not think about anything, but our whole will is directed toward the highest things, and our soul is set ablaze with the fire of the Holy Spirit." In the silence our soul is nourished, and God speaks to our hearts. Rolle goes on to say, "I used to delight indeed to sit alone, so that away from all the racket, my song could flow more easily. With heartfelt fervor, I would feel the sweetest joy, and undoubtedly I received this as a gift from him, him whom I have loved above all things and beyond description."

Each evening as the last rays of sunlight beamed across the woodland floor, I knew that I would have to leave my spot at the edge of the trees and return to a world much less contemplative in nature; but when I did return, it was always with a renewed sense of peace. And as I left the woods and reentered the affairs of daily living, my conversation, my sweet communion with God, did not stop. The time that we spent together made it easier for me to draw upon his presence any time of the day. Regardless of the circumstances, I found I could seek him out. At first, I cherished the time we spent together and returned to the woods as often as I could in order to spend even more time in his presence, As time passed, though, I occasionally found myself asking him what he thought about a particular matter; before long I realized I had begun to take everything before him.

I wondered, *Is this what it would be like to live a life of prayer? Could we pray without ceasing? Can we live every moment in his presence and be assured that he is hearing our every word?* In answer to these musings, God returned me to his simple yet perfect words of worship: the Lord's Prayer. He took the prayer of my youth, which seemed irrelevant to me at the time, and began to explain its greatness to me, showing me how rich and full his model prayer was. Perfect in every way and simple enough to keep with us always. (You may have noticed that throughout *Springtime of the Soul* I quote from the New King James Version of the Bible, for its poetic beauty and the graceful arrangement of the words stir my heart. For the Lord's Prayer, however, I revert to the language of the King James Version. At the time of my childhood, the New Testament had not yet been revised, so the wording in the King James Version is what I learned and what I still hold dear.)

As scripture says, "Therefore, pray":

Our Father which art in heaven,
Hallowed be thy name.
Thy kingdom come,
Thy will be done in earth, as it is in heaven.
Give us this day our daily bread.
And forgive us our debts, as we forgive our debtors.
And lead us not into temptation,
but deliver us from evil: For thine is the kingdom,
and the power, and the glory, for ever. Amen.

· MATTHEW 6: 9–13 ·

The phrases themselves speak to me of living a life of prayer:

> *Our Father*—I give thanks to my heavenly Father, who knew me in my mother's womb, created me in his image, and desires nothing less than an intimate relationship with me. I no longer have to question who I am, for I am his beloved, claimed by him, made pure and holy by him, to carry out his sacred purpose here on earth.

> *which art in heaven*—I praise him for being a God of holiness, who reigns in Heaven while also being a God in man here on Earth. He reigns above us at the same time as he reigns within us. The almighty God of our universe comes to me personally and is available for me any moment of the day. Remaining in his presence is where I place my hope and my heart.

> *Hallowed be thy name*—I stand in awe of the mystery of his presence within me and am assured of his concern for my righteousness, peace, and joy in the holy spirit. Let me walk worthy of his calling, and let others see him in me. I hope his light shines in all I do.

Thy kingdom come—I pray that God's kingdom, his holy spirit, will enter into me and that I will continue to desire the promise of the Father to live within me.

Thy will be done in earth, as it is in heaven—"Thy will be done, thy will be done" will be a reminder throughout my life of the night I cried out to him, seeking him, willing to turn my life over to him. Being sure of God's love, I can submit my life daily to his plan for me. I pray that I will be obedient and go about his work— promptly, readily, and cheerfully.

Give us this day our daily bread—I live in the assurance that God will give me just what I need for the day. I will trust in his divine providence, learn to trust him with the future, thank him for the past, and rejoice in the present. And I will remember that what he has given goes with me into the world for the sake of others.

And forgive us our debts, as we forgive our debtors—God has forgiven me of my wrongdoings, and I pray that he will give me the love to forgive others. I ask him for grace to understand the conditions of my fellow man and not to judge too quickly.

And lead us not into temptation, but deliver us from evil—I pray for protection for myself and others, for the opportunity to stay close to Jesus so I can remain pure in heart and not be tempted to compromise my thoughts and actions.

For thine is the kingdom, and the power, and the glory, for ever—I praise and acknowledge the omnipresence of God and rejoice in the glory of knowing him and living each day to the fullest because of his presence in my life.

Amen—It is well with my soul.

I hear this prayer with far greater appreciation today and no longer recite the words mindlessly; these phrases now have significant meaning to me as I speak them. Often, as I slowly recite the Lord's Prayer, I get lost in the beauty that it holds for me.

Yes, we can live a life of prayer, for prayer is God's gift of himself to each of us, his vow to be readily available to us at all times. Imagine living as though we were in continual conversation—behind the scenes, beneath the surface—with our Creator. Living in such a way that we did not "save up" that sense of intimacy with the heavenly Father for those few times a day when we engage in a more formal prayer, but rather that we participate in an ongoing internal dialogue—prayer—with him. Our thoughts and our actions would be completely pure in motive. We would live a life of continual peace and joy, letting nothing stand in our way or hinder our beloved relationship. Our hearts would be truly pure. But we must believe that God will answer prayer, or we cannot pray. He will do what he promises us, but we must believe. We must be willing to put our trust in him.

I will always remember the day that God showed me His magnificent power. I was driving to work after church one Sunday, and I felt that God was encouraging me to drive around our family business and pray for both the safety of the people working there and for the facility. How odd it seemed to me. Not surprisingly, I lamented about this unusual task, which seemed unimportant at the time, but I did as he requested. I drove around the building and prayed on my way to work. Only a few days later I was to witness his unlimited goodness. A mini-tornado came through our area, uprooting trees, causing power outages, and doing structural damage to the homes surrounding our business, but the severe winds did not harm our facility at all.

On the day when we were dealing with the chaotic weather, I had no time to think about what God had asked me to do earlier in the week. Only when I went to bed that night did I remember what I had done the Sunday before. I was overwhelmed, to say the least. Our rational mind tries to explain away this kind of phenomenon as merely coincidental. Or perhaps we say that we were just fortunate the storm missed us. But in my heart, having experienced God's intervention firsthand and seen his response, I believe it was a miracle.

We read about miracles that occurred in biblical times, and we think of them as a part of history; we are reluctant to consider the possibility that they can actually happen today. But why not today? Our God is alive and well and still performing miracles. *What if I had not followed God's request for me to drive around our facility and pray? What if I had ignored his whispering voice?* At that time I found it hard to believe that he called upon *me* to do his work. Me—ordinary, far from perfect, still lacking so much, in just the early stages of learning to trust in him. Yet he chose *me* to do his work.

How God answers prayer is too marvelous for me to understand. I believe in him because I have experienced the wonders of his mighty works; I simply needed to be ready and willing to follow. I will never question what seems out of the ordinary again. I will never tarry in my response to him. He has my full and undivided attention in all that he chooses to place before me.

The answers for my life come entirely out of my prayer time. There have been times when I was uncertain of what to do, what decision to make, until I sought his help and things came clearly into perspective. I welcomed handing all matters over to God. He always has a far better answer than I have, and I continue to hold tightly to them. There is such freedom in being able to release my concerns to God in prayer. No wonder that Jesus sought him out in the morning and before the close of day. Jesus was showing us how to remain in fellowship with God. Though a very public figure in his day, Jesus came to God privately and sought him out for all things. He would pray and then go out into the world. That's the way Jesus did it: he sought out his Father and then went about his work.

My new life with God began with a very simple prayer. There was nothing complicated about the words he gave me, and yet, through his power, those words had a transforming effect on my life. The possibility of this transformation is the mystery of his unconditional love for us. We have a tendency to complicate the simplicity of prayer, looking for techniques or formulas that will help us pray more efficiently, more successfully. But it is purely a matter of coming before God with the single, simple desire of being with him, to empty ourselves completely of the needs of the world around us and to focus on him. I did not know that the greatest work of our lives is prayer and that prayer itself is an ongoing conversation between the lover and his beloved.

I thank him for his gift and am warmed by the thought that I will rest in his love until another sunset catches my eye and once again I will be drawn along the wooded path into the beauty of his presence. To this day I cannot he with him without tears. I think of them as my liquid prayer. It was through my tears that I first sought him out. It is through my tears that I was cleansed and purified. It is through my tears that he softened my heart and deepened my love for him. And it is through my tears that I am able to express my joy at being able to sit in his presence. May my tears continue to flow as rivers of water renewing life for myself as well for those for whom they are shed.

"When you pray, go into your room,
and when you have shut the door,
pray to your Father
who is in the secret place;
and your Father who sees in secret
will reward you openly."

· MATTHEW 6:6 ·

The Daffodil Principle

The perfectly formed embryonic flower, which was encased within the bulb and surrounded by layers of nourishing tissue, has become visible, and is unfurling beneath the warmth of the sun. Light influences the growth of a flower by its quantity and quality. The more sunlight a plant receives, the better it is able to produce food. And the light quality encourages flowering. Scientists have discovered that it is not the length of the light period that triggers a plant's growth, but the length of uninterrupted dark periods.

It is important that we protect our hearts with a depth of prayer that will strengthen and support us in our growth. May we remember that we need uninterrupted periods, solely with our Creator, to help us come into full bloom.

Blooming

The Mighty One, God the Lord,
Has spoken and called the earth
from the rising of the sun to its going down.
Out of Zion, the perfection of beauty,
God will shine forth.

• PSALM 50:1, 2 •

101

A JOURNAL EXCERPT

Dear Father,

I awake desiring you. Some wait for the new dawn, but I wait for you. How great is your love! You loved me, waited patiently for me, and brought forth all that you created. You saw potential in me that I did not know existed, a beauty of character hidden beneath many layers. You brought me out of the barrenness of life and placed me in fertile soil. You nourished me with your many blessings of love and friendship and showed me the path for my growth. You became my friend and walked with me down this path of life, guiding and directing my steps, not allowing them to falter along life's rocky road. You have provided for my every need, giving more than I even realized at times. You are truly the source and center of all that I am.

With all that you have done, I feel a need to share your treasures with others so that they, too, may come to know you and the riches that you have waiting for them. But how? How do I speak of a love so grand? Words just don't seem sufficient or marvelous enough to express my gratitude. Do our actions speak louder than our words? Is how we live our lives a greater show of our faith than what we say about it? Imagine our impact on others if we could speak about our faith as well as living it. Help me always to live my life out of my love for you.

"What can I offer you today?" I give willingly of myself, to be used by you. I surrender all that I am, for what I am is solely yours.

Our mountainside has come alive with a magnificent beauty. The daffodils are now in full bloom, and the landscape before me is aglow with the many varied shades of yellow. The rays of the morning sun dance across the butter-colored petals and magnify their loveliness. It is a sight to behold. While my eyes take in the panorama, my mind returns to the day I held the clipping from the mail-order catalogue in my hand and envisioned the possibilities for this area. It has taken several years to bring about the changes in my garden, but those changes are well worth the effort. As the wind blows in my direction, I can smell the daffodils' fragrance, delicate yet pungent. To see their heads nodding in the breeze reminds me of William Wordsworth's well-known poem:

> *I wandered lonely as a cloud*
> *That floats on high o'er vales and hills,*
> *When all at once I saw a crowd,*
> *A host, of golden daffodils;*
> *Beside the lake, beneath the trees,*
> *Fluttering and dancing in the breeze.*

Without hesitation, I reach down and pinch the stem of a nearby daffodil, then lift it up to inspect it more closely. The one I've picked is larger in size and has a trumpetlike cup with an orange center. As I hold the flower in my hand and take in the surrounding loveliness, I think back to how this mountainside looked the first time I saw it. What was once void of color and beauty is now a gardener's delight.

As I bask in a feeling of wholeness, I give thanks for what God has done in me. But mere thanks does not seem sufficient for all God's gifts of abundance and for his many acts of kindness. Do we honor him more by what we do than what we say? If our love for him is so great, we should perhaps simply let our lives speak. God saved me by his grace; now I am committed to living my life out of gratitude for all he has done for me. If we truly have allowed him to claim us as his own, then our eyes are his eyes, our feet are his feet, our hands are his hands, and our lives must reflect all that he has inspired within us. The world cannot see him, but it can see us.

So many changes had occurred for Bob and me over the past few years. We had created more balance in our lives and as a result were enjoying our hours at work as well as the time we spent outside of work. Our days were full of activities, but we were both committed to our devotions and prayer time each morning, a part of our day that we set aside just to spend with God. And as our faith grew, so did our involvement with our church. Bob was enjoying his participation in the construction of the new sanctuary and had been invited to go along on a mission trip to Guatemala. As much as he wanted to go, though, only a real act of faith would get him there: Bob had been claustrophobic since his heart attack and had not flown in several years. Our pastor encouraged him to go ahead and make arrangements to travel with the team, and he promised that they would pray together about Bob's flying concerns.

I was continuing my evening visits to the nursing home to talk with Grandma Jennie. One evening, following the death of one of her sisters, she shared with me some of the memories of the good times they'd had during their childhood. She recalled how, since they often did not have access to a car, they walked everywhere together. She spoke of the fun they had simply walking to the woods to pick arbutus, teaberries, or blueberries. They also walked to school, to church, and to the homes of neighbors. Every time they walked they sang, and in doing so they all developed wonderful singing voices. Grandma's love of singing carried over into her adult life as she sang every Sunday morning in the church choir. I have a vivid memory of sitting in the church pew, one Sunday morning after a sleep-over, and listening to both my grandparents sing in the choir. Until that evening with Grandma Jennie, I'd had no idea where her love of music had come from. I loved hearing her stories, and the hours flew by as I sat by her side listening to her sweet voice share stories of her past. And I adored seeing her eyes light up as she recalled those events of her youth.

Having experienced the joy of spending time with God, there were times I wanted nothing more than to remain with him, to rest in his presence, to be blessed by his love and sweetness. I took such comfort from being with him and had no desire to venture elsewhere. Such beauty surrounded me on our mountaintop that I could think of nothing other than staying right here on Daffodil Hill, avoiding all further life tests and tribulations. I imagined how peaceful life would be, living in seclusion and not needing to confront the demands and responsibilities of everyday life. If I had to reenter the world, perhaps I could select a safe haven where everyone held the same beliefs, where no conflict existed and only harmony reigned.

Finding a place of repose, where we can from time to time rest and renew ourselves, is very important; these periods give God an excellent opportunity to work within us. We must carve out and protect time for our souls in order to stay connected with and to nourish our bodies. We cannot give what we do not have, so we must first fill ourselves to overflowing before we can attempt to give to others. Eventually, however, we must venture off the mountain, travel down into the valley, and take our place among other members of society to do the work that is waiting for us.

A friend reminded me of our need to come down from the mountain when he said, "God does not take us on the journey just to enjoy the scenery." I'm sure God does not want us to miss the beauty of all that he has placed around us for our enjoyment, but there is real work that needs to be done here on Earth. Whether we are called by vocation or avocation, God asks us to be his partners in the work that exists on this planet. He could easily do it himself, but he desires our participation. I don't want my faith to be self-contained, reserved only for my personal benefit; rather, I want to be a true follower of Jesus, one who serves mankind and contributes meaningfully to society, using the many talents God has given me. The paradox of our faith is that while we must do the early work in private, God then asks us to take it public. It's not enough to seek him for ourselves; we must, just as Jesus did, take who we are, and what God has done within us, and share it with those whom we encounter.

Years ago, I remember picking up an old Bible that was dated 1887. Though I no longer recall where I was or the circumstances at the time, I remember being struck by the age and the immense size of the book. As I opened the book, my eyes caught the words someone had elegantly inked onto the inside of the cover, "Faithful Unto Death." I repeated the words softly to myself, and thought, I want someone to be able to write those same words in my Bible at the end of my earthly stay. *"Faithful Unto Death." What would that kind of life look like? What would "living by faith" mean?* There was a time when I did not understand what faith meant, let alone what it might mean to *live* by faith. I remember writing the question in my journal, *"What is faith?" Was it a surrender of will? Was it a movement away from self? Was it a question about trust?*

Faith, originating from the Greek word *pistis* meaning "trust," is an act of trust for God and ourselves: He is entrusting us with his work on Earth, and we are entrusting him with our lives.

> As Hadewijch of Antwerp wrote: "O dear child! The best possible life is this: to do our utmost to content God with love, and above all trust in Him. For we come closest to Him by confidence; for true prayer is nothing else than pure abandonment to him, with perfect fidelity to trust him in all that he is.…Take care that God be honored by you and by all those whom you can help, with effort, with self-sacrifice, with counsel, and with all that you can do" (*Spiritual Formation Bible*).

The faith we hold, when expressed to others, becomes an outward representation of God's work within us. God established inside us a basis for faith; by answering my call to him the night of Bob's heart attack, he was doing so within me. As our faith strengthens, we find our desire to follow the commands of the one who healed us—the one who taught us about love, about prayer, about spirituality—increasing. Throughout the process, as we go about the work that God gives us, our ordinary lives become sacred: We conduct our lives out of gratitude for all he has done, we live from his divine love for others, we take all things before him in prayer.

We can read about God's early servants and their experiences with faith in Hebrews 11:

By faith we understand that the universe was formed
    at God's command.

By faith Abel offered God a better sacrifice.

By faith Enoch was taken from this life.

By faith Noah built an ark.

By faith Abraham obeyed and went.

By faith Isaac blessed Jacob and Esau.

By faith Jacob blessed each of Joseph's sons.

By faith Joseph spoke of the exodus.

By faith Moses' parents hid him.

By faith Moses led his people.

All of these early believers lived out their love of God; they were strong in the Lord, mighty in prayer, and rich in their faith. It wasn't enough for them merely to know God, accepting what he had done in them; they heard his command for their lives and—not always knowing the results— acted with obedience, living out of the integrity of their souls and following his call for their lives. These great men of faith had learned how to hear him in the silence, and they spent their lives waiting on the Lord's direction. When he provided that direction, they were willing to go wherever he called them. What a show of their trust and faith. How pleased God must have been to see their love for him exhibited in their lives. They changed the fate of man by their desire and willingness to respond to God's command.

God showed up in the ordinariness of their lives just as he does in ours, and it is in that ordinariness where we find opportunities to do his work. Oswald Chambers says, "There is nothing thrilling about a laboring man's work, but it is the laboring man who makes the conceptions of the genius possible; and it is the laboring saint who makes the conceptions of his Master possible." God claims our body, mind, and soul, and by his grace he fills our spirit, first giving us a new consciousness of who we are, and then filling us with a desire to do his will. I desire nothing less than to be one of his followers. Could I perhaps be a disciple like John? If we are wholly his, we must go out and do the work to which he calls us. If we hear his call and we do not follow his command, then it follows that we do not believe. Our faith is empty if it produces no result upon the life we live.

Faith exercises power over our lives; it leads us to serve God in our daily calling. Jesus says, "If anyone serves Me, let him follow Me…" (John 12:26), in other words, showing obedience to the divine command is the way to show love for Jesus. Faith leads us to exhibit the spirit of Christ to exhibit the spirit of Christ in what we ordinarily do, showing all courtesy, gentleness, forbearance, charity, and grace. We should do all ordinary work with an eye to demonstrating his glory and his character.

Faith allows us to seek God's help in whatever vocation he places us. We can pray to God for strength as a mother, a skilled technician, an artist, a student. Regardless to what we commit, if we bring everything before God, if we have faith that all matters rest in his hands, our hearts will be quieted.

Faith exercises a beneficial influence upon our day-to-day lives, for it reconciles us to any discomforts that may be part of our calling. Not every divine command is easy or lucrative. Faith gives us the courage to carry on even when our days are difficult. God knew we would face daily struggles, which is why he wanted us to have him close at hand, readily available to us when we need to call upon him.

Faith has yet another effect upon ordinary life—it casts all our day-to-day burdens upon the Lord. God promises to lift our yoke, if we are willing to let him carry it. We will find contentment in all we do by seeking God's help throughout our day with all matters that lie before us, carrying his constant shield of protection with us, and at the close of our day, we can empty out all the gathered troubles of our day, and fall asleep with the peace of knowing they will rest with him.

Faith has a happy influence upon our present life, for it eases the expectations that we place upon ourselves. If we follow the command given to us by our Father, then we need not worry about the opinions and judgments of those around us, for the direction of our lives comes from above, rather than from man, providing us with a peace of mind.

Faith is a precious preparation for anything and everything that comes our way, we must be sure it accompanies us everywhere. It should be our companion in the home and in the marketplace. Faith is for every place in which we find ourselves.

This omnipotent God of ours found me in the ordinary setting of my life, breathed new life into me, and called me forth to do his work. From that day on, everything was different. It wasn't that life itself had changed—I faced the same daily challenges as before—but I had changed. He had given me a new set of eyes with which to view the world and a renewed heart that was open to his love and teachings. Our walk together was a bit awkward at first because I did not understand how he would begin speaking to me and directing my life. There were times I thought perhaps I was receiving his direction, but how could I be sure? Sometimes I heard a quiet voice speaking within me, yet I found myself wondering if this was my voice or his.

His soft whisperings often came when I least expected them, without warning and not always with the most convenient timing. Occasionally his requests seemed irrational. At times, I would think I heard his voice giving me a little nudge toward a particular action, and I would continue to pursue my own agenda, but he would remain persistent, returning often to remind me of his command. He was relentless when I did not hear or could not understand, and only when I filled his command was my soul content.

As the basis for my faith strengthened, those early days

became a proving ground for our love. He would make a simple request, and—even though I did not necessarily understand the "why" of his asking—I would follow through with the task, as insignificant as it sometimes seemed. Our partnership evolved into one based on giving and receiving. Once I understood his request, I would put forth my effort. Before long, during my time before him every morning, I would find myself asking him what he wanted of me and how I could best serve him. In return, he would give me just what I needed for my day, be it patience or understanding, insight or clarity.

As graceless as my first steps were, we continued in our efforts to match our stride, and slowly our steps synchronized. I gradually accepted his presence in all that I did, believing that what he had planned for me was far greater than what I had planned for myself. I was learning to live my life out of my time with him, walking with him day by day, hour by hour, minute by minute—and obeying his every command. In time, I focused less on me and more on God, losing my "self" and the demands on my life to his precious and holy commands.

Faith brings profound meaning to human existence, and it provides the answers to the questions on which all our happiness depends; true happiness cannot be reached any other way. Oswald Chambers states: "Faith is not a pathetic sentiment, but a robust, vigorous confidence built in the fact that God is our holy lover." Early on, I realized that I could never be satisfied with just a one-time glance in his direction; instead, I wanted to be able to gaze continually at the heart of God. I wanted his direction in everything; so I returned to seek him again, and again, and again.

Although we may not be able to understand the work God gives us, we can be sure that, if we agree to do his work, he will supply us with all the knowledge and wisdom required to fulfill his request and he will lift us above our daily struggles. We can rest assured that our burdens will never be too heavy to carry and that his help will always be available to us. We are not asked to be perfect in our work for him, and we are not often asked to bring about specific results; we are simply asked to be faithful, to come as we are—equipped with a genuine desire to serve him. If we do so, we will be furnished with his love, his wisdom, and his shared strength.

A friend (or, I should say, a teacher) gave me a book that he thought I would enjoy. It was *Curate's Awakening* written by George MacDonald, who authored many books during the late 1800s. He was a novelist whom even C. S. Lewis regarded as a master. In the chapter titled Genuine Service, two men engage in conversation about what real service is. This is what one of the characters of the book has to say:

> *I believe that true and genuine service may*
> *be given to the living God. And for the*
> *development of the divine nature in man, it*
> *is necessary that he should do something*

for God. And it is not hard to discover how, for God is in every creature and in their needs. Therefore, Jesus says that whatever is done to one of his little ones is done to him. And if the soul of a believer be the temple of the Spirit, then is not the place of that man's [or woman's] labor—his shop, his bank, his laboratory, his school, his factory—the temple of Jesus Christ, where the spirit of the man is at work? Mr. Drew, your shop is the temple of your service where the Lord Christ ought to be throned. Your counter ought to be his alter, and everything laid on it with intent of doing as you can for your neighbor, in the name of Christ Jesus.

It is my hope and prayer that we would each realize opportunities in our daily life to provide genuine service. That our true spirit would come alive in the midst of the work God gives us. What a difference we could make if we saw all our labors in this fashion, if we took the fullness of ourselves, who God made us to be, into our workplaces, into our volunteer sites, into our leisure activities, into our home lives. Imagine how we could affect the lives of others if we placed God in the center of everything, living our lives out of our love for him, everywhere, every day.

One summer, while vacationing with my husband and friends, I came upon a craft shop that was selling handmade leather goods. It must have been the scent of the leather that drew me into the store. I wasn't looking for anything in particular, until my eyes fell on a leather notebook, just the size to hold a small tablet. It felt good in my hands, so I purchased it, not knowing then exactly how I would use it. But God knew. As I grew in my understanding of hearing his voice, the notebook became the place for me to record his commands for my day. Morning after morning, I waited for his gentle whisperings, and when they came I jotted them down—creating my "to do" list—to ensure that I wouldn't overlook his slightest request. The notebook, along with his commands, became my faithful companion. With each passing year the leather has become softer and smoother, just as my walk with him has also grown smoother.

Even though there is a cost to following him—a significant cost, for the things that God asks of us will not bring us worldly power or glory—I desire to live my life remaining faithful to the commands he has so graciously placed before me. I may not understand why he issues certain commands and I may not always feel comfortable not understanding, but I accept the mystery of this life, resting in his love and assurance that all will be well in his presence. When the day comes that I meet him face-to-face, he will know that I have been faithful to his work and that I have loved him with my life. In the depths of my soul, I know there is no greater love.

God having provided
something better for us,
that they should not be made perfect
apart from us.

· HEBREWS 11:40 ·

The Daffodil Principle

The word *daffodil* did not enter the English language until the 1500s. The old name for this flower was "affodyle," believed to have originated from the old English "affo dyle," which means "that which cometh early." Because the daffodil reaches the fullness of bloom during Lent, some call the flower a "Lenten lily." One legend tells that the daffodil first appeared on the night of the Last Supper, in the garden of Gethsemane, to comfort Jesus during his time of sorrow. When presenting these blooms as a gift, you should never give just one; some believe a lone daffodil is a symbol of misfortune. Always give a bunch of daffodils to ensure your recipient's happiness and joy.

God desires each of us to come into the fullness of bloom. He plants us exactly where we belong, provides all that is needed for our growth, and takes great pleasure in seeing our beauty come forth. May we live our lives through our love for him.

Multiplying

But the mercy of the Lord
is from everlasting to everlasting
On those who fear Him,
And His righteousness to children's children,
To such as keep His covenant,
And to those who remember
His commandments to do them.

• PSALM 103:17,18 •

Dear Father,

With each new day, you bring me your love, and I continue to seek you and remain in you, for it is in your presence that my spirit is renewed. You have helped me to remember those early days in my search for you and the passion of my soul, so desperately in need. You brought me much more than I was searching for and filled me with the desires of my heart.

I pray, as my faith continues to grow, that I will keep the childlike wonder present when I first came to you, that my soul's thirst will continue to be quenched by you, that my heart will be open to love those around me, that my mind will remain eager and willing to learn the new things you have to teach me, that my ears will be tuned to your soft whisperings, that my mouth will speak of your many blessings, that my eyes will be open to behold the wonders of this world, and that my hands and feet will be forever willing to follow your commands.

Thank you for being the sanctuary of my soul, for allowing me to live in communion with you throughout my journey here on Earth. You have protected me and guided me through the storms of my life, bringing me peace and joy. It is here that you are preparing me for a lifetime with you—I like to think of it as my readiness for eternity. You have already provided such abundance in my life that I dare not think what splendors you have waiting for me; the mere thought of it brings me great hope for the future!

As I make my rounds this morning, there are signs that spring is slowly giving way to summer. The flowering pear, which had been so full of white blossoms this past week, is turning green and the dogwood trees are starting to sprinkle their pale colors of white and pink amid our woods. There are still a few daffodil blooms scattered along our mountainside, but for the most part they have withered and dried upon their stems. I always wanted to rid my garden of the spent flowers until I learned that the bulbs need the nutrients from their stems to feed next year's growth.

I've learned, too, that once a bulb is planted and begins to take root, it quickly multiplies. Within a few years, it can amass quite a large cluster of bulbs. I have, in fact, already dug up sixty to eighty bulbs that ultimately formed from a single planting. To avoid overcrowding and to promote better growth, it is best to dig up the bulbs, separate them, and dry them in readiness for the next season's planting. If you followed this procedure each year, you'd likely never have to buy another bulb, for once a single bulb becomes established, there will be clusters to dig up.

My joy each fall is finding new locations to plant my prolific daffodils. For years, I limited my planting to our mountainside, wanting so much to increase the beauty right outside my door; then I discovered that planting them in locations where others could be blessed by their beauty gave me even greater joy. Each year, as the planting season nears, new possibilities come to mind: the side yard of a new house built by a family member, a garden started by a new acquaintance who has entered my life. It is even more fun if I can plant the bulbs without the recipients' awareness, so that, when spring arrives, they will be totally surprised when the newcomer makes an appearance.

As the days become warmer, and I realize that summer is not far off, it saddens me that this beautiful season of new growth and freshness is coming to an end. I know that I will welcome the coming season for all of its own particular beauty, but spring will always remain my favorite. Every year, when it once again arrives, I am given the opportunity to revisit the glory of God's saving grace in my life, the rebirth of my soul. I do not feel that I am nearer to God during this season than I am at any other, but those days are a reminder of his continuing work in my life, and they are a time for me to reflect on and give thanks for all that God has done within me. Out of my cry, he brought me life. Out of my pain, he helped me to realize my greatest need. And out of his promise, he delivered the greatest love I would ever know.

Seven years after Bob had his heart attack and open-heart surgery, he failed his annual stress test. I knew it wasn't good news when he returned so quickly from the hospital that day. After further testing, the doctors confirmed the need for another open-heart procedure. Neither of us was thrilled with the prospect of going through this ordeal a second time around, however, because we now had our faith to support and guide us, we were much better equipped to handle the situation this time than we had been before. We were also sustained by our church family and their prayers. On the day of the procedure, our family and I waited with our pastor and several friends from the church. There were a few rough days immediately following the surgery, but Bob's recovery went extremely well. I know that we were covered by the prayers of many. How much we appreciated the visits from numerous people we had come to know and love. It was definitely a testimony of faith to go through a second time the same sort of hardship, yet to experience it from such another perspective. Having God with us made all the difference.

My trips to the nursing home were eventually ended by Grandma Jennie's death, which was precipitated by a fall she took while helping one of the other residents. She died the way she had lived her life—helping others in need. My last visit to her room was to pack up her few possessions. The items that struck my heart as I picked them up were her Bible and her shoes. I thought of the countless times I had entered her room to find her asleep, her Bible lying open on her lap. She must have dozed off during her quiet moments with the Lord. And as I packed up her shoes I acknowledged that, even though they were quite small, it would take a lot to fill them. I can still hear her voice: "Remember, it's really all about eternal life." I have now come full circle, from personal denial of my own mortality to the assurance and acceptance of a life everlasting.

The night of Bob's heart attack, we were fearful of the future. Although we had our wills in order we did not have our lives in order. We had spent a lot of time on the things of this earthly world and very little time on the things of *God's* world. We were fearful of the future, because we had nothing to look forward to beyond what we knew existed here on Earth. But our relationship with God has given us the promise of eternal life.

Eternal life shall be ours. But what is eternal life, and how do we achieve it? According to Jesus, "And this is eternal life, that they may know You, the only true God, and Jesus Christ whom You have sent" (John 17:3). Eternal life is reached through establishing a personal friendship with God, getting to know him on an intimate basis. It is more than simply studying the historical details surrounding the story of Jesus' life. Rather, it is the pursuit of supernatural knowledge, what we gain through a close, devoted relationship with the Lord. As with any friend, a relationship can deepen only by being in continual communication with each other. It may seem too easy, but we can have the promise of eternal life simply by coming to know the one true God. And to know him, we must surrender our will for his will and learn to trust him with our life.

Jesus came from God, did his work here on Earth, and returned to God, just as we are asked to do. We are placed on this Earth, for whatever time we are given, to prepare to be with him for eternity. Life holds far greater purpose once we understand that when our work is done on Earth, we will simply transition to another place in time. C. S. Lewis said, "Aim for Heaven and you will get earth 'thrown in': aim at earth and you will get neither." We should aim for Heaven while we are still on Earth. God is here as well as in Heaven. The very ground we walk on is his, as is everything we see and touch, so let us acknowledge all matter of being as sacred and treat it with honor.

Our time here on Earth is sacred. We need to guard and protect our time and how we use it. Our time here is very short and precious; we can squander it so easily pursuing things that have no substance beyond this world. God promises us eternity, but life on this Earth is limited. How we spend eternity is based on what we do here. The life we lead on Earth is merely a transition period, during which we may prepare to receive his greatness for all time. We spend a lot of time, money, and effort preparing for a career or profession; are we spending as much time preparing for how we spend eternity?

We should put our time and effort into useful and spiritual purposes. There is great work to do here: children to love and provide for, friends to support, the poor to relieve. We have diseases to cure and discoveries to make. We have difficulties to master and many obligations to fulfill, our private and public concerns and duties of the world. All of these things we do as a perpetual service to God, and what we learn and experience through it all is preparing us for eternity. Not only should we serve him in our work, but we must set aside quiet time to address the needs of our soul. We cannot run on empty.

Our intentions should be holy. To ensure that we approach our actions with the right purpose and a pure motive, we should first reflect upon their end result. Will our plan have a positive influence not only on the here and now but on the future? We generally tend to think about finding a "quick fix"; instead, we must focus on how our actions will affect lives over the next year, the next decade, the next century, and into eternity. If, before we acted, we were to think twice about the impact of our deeds on others, we would certainly move with greater care. When we precede our actions by seeking out God first and asking if our plan will bring him glory, then we are acting with the right purpose and a pure motive. Then we can be assured that the results of our actions will be good for eternity.

His presence is in all things. The first gleam of heaven is already inside us. God is present in the hearts of all people; by his holy spirit, there is his kingdom. God is present in our conscience and in our manner of life. He is present in every thought, word, and deed. He is no stranger to the lives we lead, either in public or in private. He is all encompassing, infinite, and we are wrapped in his very nature.

As Christians we are to be eternally hopeful. Knowing all that God has done for us here, we can be confident of our future, even of the things we cannot see or know. Throughout life, about some things we will be in a continual state of "unknowing." Although he has lifted the veil for us on a portion of the mystery surrounding him, more revelations lie ahead. But if we have learned to trust him in this earthly world, then we will trust in his world, the world that awaits us.

We should live lives of joy and peace, resting in his assurance. We should rejoice and be glad in the midst of apparent misfortune or seeming sadness, knowing that he will work out all things for the good. He is in direct control of what we cannot see or understand, and we are to look for his light to shine in all circumstances. Let us desire, pray for, and long for God's glory, that is, the great ending of our flesh but the gaining of our soul. We must not view this ending as a matter of physical death, but as the inclination toward self-sacrifice. His hope brings great joy.

God, in his perfection, has left no stone unturned with me. He took everything I did not know and began to show me the answers. He gave me just what I needed. How could I not have the greatest confidence in a God who has supported me throughout my growth? How could I not have the greatest confidence in a God who has helped carry the burdens of my life? How could I not trust in a God who has fused my will with his will? How could I not trust in a God who has given me wisdom through his Spirit?

And if those were not enough to convince me of my future, how could I not believe in a God who showed me his love—a love that permeated my very being and healed me from within, a love that helped me to heal all of my earthly relationships. He began our relationship with an irrevocable covenant—a promise of an everlasting relationship, existing from here through eternity.

There is no doubt that he is present with us on Earth. I cannot see him, but I have certainly felt his presence innumerable times. He is not visible to the human eye, but the soul knows deep within that he is in everything. I cannot walk the grounds around our home without thinking; this is where he met me; this is where we spoke; and this is where he taught me to pray. Yes, I definitely trust him with my future. He has proven himself over and over again.

I may not know what is in my future, but I can trust that, whatever it may be, it is exactly what I need in this life to prepare me to spend eternity with him. He is making me ready for the world that lies beyond. I believe in this world, that which I have never experienced, because I have seen God's spiritual existence here on Earth.

He claimed my heart, mind, and soul. We came to know each other intimately, and even though I have not seen his face, I will know him when I see him. I will know my lover by the sweet resonance of his voice, the voice that comes to me every morning in the dark and whispers in my ear throughout the day. I will know him by the gentleness of his spirit, which is present within me. And I am sure that I will not have to go looking for him, for he will be waiting for me, just as he did early in our journey.

May we desire to seek him so that we can experience the joy of knowing him right here on Earth. We are here but for a short while; then, if we let our Creator guide the way, we will travel the unknown path back to him, back to our source of life, our eternal home, where we will experience total wholeness. It will be a day of great reunion and total completion. I'm sure the Heavens will break forth with triumphant joy on that day!

We, as believers, must submerge ourselves in God and let others know of the gift of love that awaits them. We must be ready to spend time with those who follow, for they, too, need to find the strength to carry on his work here on Earth. We must encourage them in their growth, seeking first to understand where they are, and then, without judgment, guiding them. We must speak of the God we know, the God who transformed us from who we were into who he knew we could become. We must witness for them what God has done within us and share the stories of our faith. We must tell the stories of God's healing power. We must tell the stories of his teaching and guidance in our lives. We must tell them what a joy it is to experience the goodness of his love and the delight in following his commands.

On the night she died, Grandma Jennie handed me her cross necklace, which she had worn for a good portion of her life. For years it hung from the corner of her picture, displayed on my wall, but recently I felt the need to wear it myself. As I fastened the chain around my neck, it seemed that I was accepting the handing off of a baton, the baton of faith being passed from one generation to another—Grandma Jennie's way of passing along the work that needed to be done by my generation.

As my fingers touch the tiny cross, I wonder how often she held it in her own grasp. I picture her holding it as she prayed for us, perhaps bringing it to her lips to softly kiss this symbol of the redeemer of her own soul. She had no idea of the legacy she left behind. This grand lady, this special saint, learned the true essence of life. She came to know her Father in a personal way. What she experienced and read, she lived. What a great example she was for all of us. I am forever grateful for her love of me, of our family, and of the Lord.

As I look at a picture of my grandchildren, one of whom is named after Grandma Jennie, I think of the work that lies ahead for me to make sure they know the stories that have brought me closer to God. That the life I live in Christ is nothing that I did myself; I simply got up and walked into the dark of night, where he met me and welcomed me into his arms. God granted me grace and mercy during my searching years, never giving up on me. When he heard the question "Is this all there is?," he began a miracle in me.

I want my grandchildren to know that the God of yesterday is the God of today and will remain for them the God of tomorrow. My prayer is that they, too, will become one of God's daffodils and will welcome him into their lives, allowing him to nourish that which he created and bring them into a fullness of life, to live in the freedom and radiance of his love, a love that will make a difference in their workplaces, their volunteer sites, their leisure activities, their home lives.

They need to hear that he is both a "then" God and a "now" God—both the God of history and the God of today. He is the reigning God of all generations. The God who instructed Noah to build the boat and save his family is the same God who parted the Red Sea for Moses as he led his people to freedom, the same God who reached out to me when I called to him the night of Bob's heart attack, the same God who spared our business from devastation when a hurricane moved through our community. We have an obligation to him to pass along the stories of our love, of our journeys to faith. If we don't, the next generation of believers will never hear them. It is up to us to share our stories and to bring God to life for those coming behind.

They need to realize that they, the next generation, represent a symbol of hope, that they will grow, bloom, and multiply. They are next to grow in the Lord, to have opportunities to live their lives to the fullest, to become all that God has planned for them.

As I put the finishing touches on this book and bid you good-bye, I see that the days are growing colder, and I still have a few more bulbs to plant. The last of the geese are honking overhead, finding their way to warmer climates, and I must prepare for the springtime that lies ahead. Surely the Lord is in this place.

One generation shall praise Your works to another,
And shall declare Your mighty acts.
I will meditate on the glorious splendor of Your majesty,
And on Your wondrous works.
Men shall speak of the might of Your awesome acts,
And I will declare Your greatness.
They shall utter the memory of Your great goodness,
And shall sing of Your righteousness.

· PSALM 145:4-7 ·

The Daffodil Principle

The way in which bulbs are propagated depends on their structure. True bulbs, using the nutrients from their stems, form "offsets" from the mature bulb. These, in turn, will grow into mature bulbs themselves when separated from the parent bulb. Even though daffodils are beautiful and seemingly fragile, in fact they remain hardy and multiply with abandon when given the proper care. Digging up the bulbs, dividing them, and finding new locations for them is important to their continued new growth. If the offsets are left in the same spot, eventually the bulb clusters will produce smaller or noticeably fewer blooms. The cycle of growth is never complete: a bulb produces a lovely flower, which then withers and dies, only to be used for food that will help form the next generation of bulbs.

The daffodil, besides being one of the early bloomers of the season and a herald of spring, is a symbol of hope, that which we yearn for but cannot see. It is the expectation of things to come, the anticipation of the future. God is hope for all who believe. He is a blessing on his sacred ground, for he will transform the troubles of this world into the reality of eternal life.

Epilogue

But as for me, I trust in You, O Lord;
I say, "You are my God."

• PSALM 31:14 •

It's been almost two years since Bob and I made our mission trip to Guatemala. It was an incredible trip for us in many ways. I still stand in awe of the many lessons God taught me during our travels. Even in the midst of sometimes unfavorable times, he protected us against harm and revealed his many truths: that we can be stripped of all our worldly possessions and yet remain rich in God's love; that he remains in control of our lives and continues to bless us abundantly.

I was baptized as an infant, which was the traditional sacrament of my church background, and always felt that one baptism was sufficient. I knew, in my heart, that my personal relationship with the Lord was enough for me, and so I never felt inclined to consider a second baptism as an adult. Once baptized, always baptized, was my thinking. But something happened on the way up that mountain as we traveled that day, listening to the stories and hearing the stories of spiritual encounters our host shared. I felt I was being nudged to take my faith public. And when I saw the beauty of the Lake Atitlán area, the thought came to me: If I were to be baptized again, this was where I would want it to occur. God had given me a new life in Christ, and I wanted to confess my faith and my commitment before other believers of our church family.

Later in the week, I had just that opportunity. I couldn't help but think, as we gathered there along the bank of the lake, how wonderful it was to make the decision to be baptized as an adult, fully aware of the meaning it holds. God had blessed me with his love, and, as a follower of Christ, I wanted to commit to my continued growth in my faith, to continue to grow into the fullness of his image. The God who called me into his fellowship is and remains faithful. My baptism in Guatemala will be a reminder to me always to seek God's will as I strive to live a life of holiness of heart and mind.

Further Reading

The Holy Bible. Any version that speaks to your heart.

Chambers, Oswald. *Daily Readings from My Utmost for His Highest.* Nashville, Tenn.: T. Nelson Publishers, 1992.

Fox, Emmet. *The Sermon on the Mount: The Key to Success in Life.* San Francisco: HarperSanFrancisco, 1992.

Jones, J. D. *The Apostles of Jesus: Studies in the Character of the Twelve.* Grand Rapids, Mich.: Kregel Publications, 1992.

Jones, Timothy (ed). *Spiritual Formation Bible: Growing in Intimacy with God Through Scripture: New Revised Standard Version.* Grand Rapids, Mich.: Zondervan Publishing, 1999.

Keating, Thomas. *The Human Condition: Contemplation and Transformation.* New York: Paulist Press, 1999.

Lewis, C. S. *Mere Christianity.* New York: Macmillan, 1952.

Merton, Thomas. *Opening the Bible.* Philadelphia: Fortress Press, 1986.

Nouwen, Henri J. M. *Life of the Beloved: Spiritual Living in a Secular World.* New York: Crossroad, 1989.

Nouwen, Henri J. M. *In the Name of Jesus: Reflections on Christian Leadership.* New York: Crossroad, 1999.

Parker, Palmer. *Let Your Life Speak: Listening for the Voice of Vocation.* San Francisco: Jossey-Bass, 1999.

About the Author

CAROLE HAMM *lives in Lewisburg, Pennsylvania, with her husband Bob and their much loved black lab. It was here they raised their two children who now live nearby raising children of their own.*

As a teenager, Carole started working in their family business, founded by her father, H. Daniel Baylor, which eventually became Country Cupboard. Started in 1963 as a farm market, the business is today a large hospitality complex including a restaurant, gift shops and hotels serving as many as 20,000 quests weekly. As the business flourished, so did Carole's career. Before retiring in 2005, she served as president of the company which provided her with the opportunity to speak about leadership, generational issues and more recently her faith. She continues to counsel the third generation of her family as they assume management of the company and is working on her second book.